About the Author

Sandra Munson is a professional home organizer in La Jolla, CA. While taking several years off to raise her two young children, she began to organize spaces for friends and family. Eventually, this passion for organization blossomed into a career. She has worked on projects with Stephanie Malcolm of room|by|ROOM inc. in residential home organization, relocation services, school site organization, and specialized media solutions.

In 2006, Sandra branched out on her own and founded her company, Harmony Home Organization. HHO is a La Jolla-based business focused on transforming a home into a clutter-free and harmonious space. She collaborates with local interior designer Celeste Trudeau to achieve the desired look and feel of a space. Sandra's areas of home organization expertise are children's spaces, home offices, and garages. She has established a reputation as an organizer who places an emphasis on green (earth-friendly) projects and budget-friendly projects. Her current client list includes both residential homes as well as local businesses.

Sandra is very active in her local public school and church. She currently serves as a volunteer on the PTO board at La Jolla Elementary and on the Children's Ministry Board at La Jolla Community Church. Creating a harmonious home has become her passion.

Dedication

I dedicate this book to my husband, Mike, who has provided me with endless love and support throughout this endeavor; my son, Jack, who makes me laugh every single day; and my daughter, Julia, who I think will walk in my footsteps.

Author's Acknowledgments

Special thanks to my parents, Nancy and Girts, for providing inspiration, information, and child care during this process; my sister Diana for being my cheerleader; my friend Stephanie for professional guidance; my friend Celeste for inspiring my confidence; my girlfriends, who are always there for support; my friend Margot for providing me with this amazing opportunity; and my photographer Tom and my stylist Sarah at Kreber.

Publisher's Acknowledgments

We're proud of this book; please send us your comments through our Dummies online registration form located at `http://dummies.custhelp.com`. For other comments, please contact our Customer Care Department within the U.S. at 877-762-2974, outside the U.S. at 317-572-3993, or fax 317-572-4002.

Some of the people who helped bring this book to market include the following:

Acquisitions, Editorial, and Media Development

Senior Project Editor: Georgette Beatty

Acquisitions Editor: Tracy Boggier

Senior Copy Editor: Elizabeth Rea

Assistant Editor: Erin Calligan Mooney

Editorial Program Coordinator: Joe Niesen

Technical Editor: Allison Shorter

Editorial Manager: Michelle Hacker

Editorial Assistant: Jennette ElNaggar

Art Coordinator: Alicia B. South

Cover Photo: Photography, Kreber/Tom Reed; Set Stylist, Kreber/Sarah Bernardi

Cartoons: Rich Tennant (`www.the5thwave.com`)

Composition Services

Project Coordinator: Katherine Crocker

Layout and Graphics: Reuben W. Davis, Erin Zeltner

Special Art: Photography, Kreber/Tom Reed; Set Stylist, Kreber/Sarah Bernardi

Proofreaders: John Greenough, Toni Settle

Indexer: Glassman Indexing Services

Publishing and Editorial for Consumer Dummies

Diane Graves Steele, Vice President and Publisher, Consumer Dummies

Kristin Ferguson-Wagstaffe, Product Development Director, Consumer Dummies

Ensley Eikenburg, Associate Publisher, Travel

Kelly Regan, Editorial Director, Travel

Publishing for Technology Dummies

Andy Cummings, Vice President and Publisher, Dummies Technology/General User

Composition Services

Gerry Fahey, Vice President of Production Services

Debbie Stailey, Director of Composition Services

Table of Contents

Introduction

Back in the day, it wasn't that challenging to maintain a tidy household because frankly, people didn't have many belongings. Your bow goes here, your arrow goes there, and you're already wearing your loincloth. Well, times have changed! We live in a consumer-based economy, meaning that clothing and products are more affordable than in past generations and, as a result, we have a lot of stuff! Enter the need for home organization.

Simply put, home organization is the process of putting away one's belongings. Is it an art or a science? Definitely both! Organization appeals to left-brained people because it's logical and systematic. But the creativity involved in selecting *how* to group things is fascinating to right-brained people. Scientists will marvel over an office's worth of items being condensed into a desk with a hutch, and artists will enjoy the satisfaction of finding just the right floral file to hold the tax returns. There's something in home organization for everyone!

Is organizing a lot of work? Probably less than you think. The process I describe in this book is very systematic and easy to follow. Basically, you assess the contents of the room, decide what items will stay and what items will go, and find the best way to display or store the items that you're keeping.

The hard work is definitely worth it. An organized home has so many benefits; immediately, you'll notice that you're saving valuable minutes because you aren't spending any time searching for missing items. With time, you'll see that you spend less money because you aren't repurchasing items that you already have. Best of all, your home will be a relaxing sanctuary that your family looks forward to returning to at the end of the day. If you're ready to create an orderly living space, *Organizing Do-It-Yourself For Dummies* is the book for you.

About This Book

My world of organization is inspired by a quote from the father of invention, Benjamin Franklin: "A place for everything and everything in its place." This quote conjures up an image of a home free of clutter and probably makes you think "I want that!" The goal of this book is to help you create harmony and order in *your* home through easy-to-apply organization techniques and do-it-yourself projects. This book gives you everything you need to tackle your house in a systematic, room-by-room method. Nothing in this book is too advanced for the average homeowner; as soon as you know how to find a wall stud and use a level, you're well on your way.

I present you with a straightforward, five-step organization plan that provides the framework necessary to transform an entire room. In those five steps, I guide you through the process of evaluating the goals of the room, identifying the limitations of the room, emptying the space and sorting, putting together projects, and reassembling the room. You're encouraged to make some tough decisions to achieve your organized home, but the result will be worth it!

While the five-step plan is the road map to get the job done, my four organization philosophies are the motivation to help keep you on track. My organization philosophies fall into four categories: be disciplined, be green, be frugal, and be clever. Organizing a room using the steps and philosophies helps you build your do-it-yourself confidence.

With the five-step plan and four organization philosophies in mind, I devote a chapter to organizing each room in your house, from the primary "work horses" of your home — entryway/living room, kitchen, bedroom/closet, bathroom, and home office — to the secondary areas of your home — kids' spaces, laundry room, and garage. In each of these chapters, I provide step-by-step directions on a wide variety of organizational projects, accompanied by full-color photos. Don't forget about the details — in each chapter, I also outline decorative finishing touches that help make your house a home. You can pick and choose the rooms you want to work on, but if you need to bring order to every part of your home, I have you covered.

Conventions Used in This Book

I include the following conventions to help you navigate this book:

- New terms appear in *italics* and are accompanied by definitions.
- All Web sites and e-mail addresses appear in `monofont`.
- Keywords in bulleted lists appear in **boldface.**
- I include extra tips and other interesting information in shaded sidebars.

Foolish Assumptions

As I wrote this book, I made some assumptions about you, dear reader:

- You want to be able to wake up in the morning to a peaceful bedroom retreat free of clutter.
- You want your clothing to fit in your closets and those closets to be organized by color and type so finding the right outfit is simple and free of frustration.
- You want to be able to cook dinner in a kitchen with streamlined cabinets and drawers and easily accessible food and appliances.
- You want to be able to easily pay your bills from your home office, quickly file documents, and locate necessary information.
- You want all of your living spaces to feel restful and clear of clutter.

How This Book Is Organized

Organizing Do-It-Yourself For Dummies is divided into four parts that deal with the preparation, execution, and finishing touches of organizing your home.

Part I: Preparing for Your Organizing Projects

What do you need to do before you get started? Begin by preparing yourself for the process both mentally and physically. By this, I mean read up on the overall process and collect all the stuff you need before you tackle a room. Great results are the byproduct of preparation, inspiration, and perspiration!

In Chapter 1, I introduce the five-step plan and four organization philosophies. They work together to motivate and guide you through all aspects of a room organization. Refer to Chapter 1 before you work on a room to get your organizational juices flowing! In Chapter 2, I present the tools necessary to complete a room; home organization relies on sorting tools, installation tools, and finishing tools. This chapter also sets time frames and expectations for your projects. By my estimate, you can transform any room in your house in fewer than 24 work-hours. Now that's motivating! In Chapter 3, I review basic carpentry terms and techniques. If I ask you to use your *carpenter's square* to make sure your shelf is perpendicular to the *stud,* knowing exactly what I'm talking about is a good idea! I also include a list of helpful frequently asked carpentry questions. Whether carpentry is brand new or old hat, I recommend reading up before starting any projects.

Part II: Organizing Primary Spaces in Your Home

How can you make your life easier? By organizing the primary spaces in your home! In this part, I provide projects for the entryway, living room, kitchen, bedroom, closets, bathroom, and home office. Take a moment to assess your biggest frustration and start in that area. If it's challenging to get dressed in the morning, begin with your bedroom closet. If the bills aren't getting paid on time, begin with the home office. If you're too frustrated to cook dinner, begin in the kitchen. Take control of your household one room at a time.

Part III: Organizing Secondary Spaces in Your Home

Secondary spaces are areas that are important to your day but aren't necessarily large living spaces. Part III provides both conventional and out-of-the-box storage ideas for your kids' spaces, laundry room, and garage. Organizing these three spaces will keep your household running like a well-oiled machine!

Part IV: The Part of Tens

A few common threads are woven into the fabric of American households: not enough time, not enough space, and needing more help! Life is busy, and you have things to do. Use the tips in this part to help your household run smoothly and save time.

Icons Used in This Book

When I have something particularly important to say in this book, I want it to jump out at you! Keep your eyes open for these icons throughout the book. They give you a heads up for potential mental notes, tips, and project pitfalls.

This icon points to important information that you should take away from this book.

This icon highlights pieces of time- and hassle-saving information.

This icon alerts you to organization pitfalls. Beware!

Where to Go from Here

This book is designed to be read from cover to cover (hint, hint), but feel free to jump right into any part or chapter depending on your needs.

Part I gives you a feel for what you need to do to prepare for a project. If you're a true organizing novice, start with this part.

Are you ready to tackle specific areas of your home? Parts II and III are where you dive into projects — organizing primary and secondary spaces of your house. When you get a few of these under your belt, you'll start to notice subtle changes in your household . . . piles of clutter have disappeared, you seem to have more leisure time, and your household feels more at peace.

If you want some easy tips and tricks to put into action right now, employ the techniques in Part IV to help your family life and your household run smoother.

Part I
Preparing for Your Organizing Projects

The 5th Wave   By Rich Tennant

"We've got to do something about the junk in this closet. There's rackets, bowls, lamps, and heaven knows how long the Harrisons have been in here."

In this part . . .

You're excited by the prospect of a clutter-free home and ready to jump into organizing a specific space, such as your kitchen or garage. Maybe you've been living with clutter for years and can't take it another day! While I applaud your enthusiasm, I strongly encourage you to read this part to find out the basics before diving into a project. Proper preparation will save you time in the long run — and you can still get started today!

In this part, I walk you through a five-step plan for organizing a room and present you with practical organizational philosophies. Mantras like "One in, one out" and "Less is more" provide inspiration as well as keep you on track during your room organizations. I also help you identify and collect your sorting, installation, and finishing tools and plan your time. Lastly, I help you brush up on your carpentry knowledge. Do you remember how to locate wall studs or ceiling joists? If you don't, I help you figure it out!

Chapter 1

The Principles of Do-It-Yourself Organization

The fact that you're reading this book signals that you're serious about organizing your home. Congratulations! There are so many perks to having an organized home — your bills get paid on time, meals are cooked quickly, and you can find your child's sleeping bag in a snap. An organized home is a direct path to an organized life!

This chapter boils down my approach to tackling a house, one room at a time. With the five-step plan, I hold your hand throughout the process — setting goals, assessing limitations, emptying and sorting, enhancing the room with projects, and reassembling the room. In addition, I present several organization philosophies to motivate and inspire you.

Five Steps to an Organized Room

Are you ready to get serious about organization? The following steps guide you through the process from beginning to end. In the long run, it saves time to approach each room with a plan. (Chapter 2 outlines an organization schedule.)

Step 1: Determine the goal of the room

You may already have a firm vision for your space. Perhaps it's from a friend's home, a TV show, or a magazine spread. Or maybe you're so frustrated by the current state of your room that you can't see the forest for the trees. In either case, I recommend spending a little time sitting in your space, assessing what you like and don't like, and envisioning the way you want it to *feel* — and function!

The goal for your space should be specific, concrete, and directly related to the function of your space. For example, the goal for your home office may be a place to manage paperwork, a desktop on which to write letters, or a space to manage your thriving home business. If you still aren't clear on your vision, make a list of exactly what you *need* to accomplish in your space, and develop this into your goal. For inspiration, search spaces online or in magazines until one jumps out at you.

Step 2: Identify the limitations of the room

Is your goal realistic? To determine the answer to this all-important question, factor in limitations such as size, layout, and requirements of the room. For example, the goal of your living room may be a welcoming space for entertaining guests. The limitations of the space may be its small size, lack of entryway, and the reality that it's the only room in the house for the home office. The fusion of the goal and its limitations is a living room with an entryway table for guests, a single sofa with an ottoman/coffee table to provide additional seating, and a discreet office nook.

Step 3: Sort the room

After you set a realistic goal for your room with the room's limitations in mind, you can empty out your room. This process is vital for organizing a space because it allows you to assess the storage needs for the items that will stay in the room.

Sort items into four large bins as follows (Chapter 2 has the details on tools):

- ✔ **STAY:** The items in this bin are in good condition, are used often, are relevant to the room's goal, and will stay in the room.
- ✔ **MOVE:** The items in this bin are in good condition and used often, but they don't belong in the room you're organizing (as related to the room's goal).
- ✔ **SHARE:** The items in this bin are in good condition but haven't been used in the last year, are duplicates of other items, or no longer serve the room's goal.
- ✔ **GO:** The items in this bin are trash — simple as that!

After the contents of your room are sorted, transfer all your MOVE items to their proper places in your home, place your SHARE items in your garage to donate at a later time, and throw away your GO items. Review your STAY items to make sure they really do support the goal of your room.

Step 4: Build and install your projects

Pat yourself on the back: After emptying and sorting the contents of your room, you now have an empty space! If you plan to paint your space, this is the opportune time because the area is cleared out and wall-mounted projects haven't been installed.

Each chapter in Parts II and III is devoted to organizing an entire room. Read up on your specific room and decide which projects are appropriate for your space. Most projects take about an hour and can be installed with a level, screwdriver, and electric drill. Some of the more advanced projects take several hours and require the use of a nail gun, carpenter's square, or ladder. (Turn to Chapter 2 for the scoop on installation tools; Chapter 3 provides details on carpentry basics.)

Step 5: Reassemble the room

Now the fun can begin! Your newly organized space will have more storage options and far fewer items. How ever did you manage before? Reinforce your commitment to an organized space by putting like items in a single container and labeling it. Add decorative accessories and a touch of whimsy to every room. I can't help but smile while I walk through my front door in July and see my Buddha statue wearing sunglasses. Then fall rolls around, and Buddha is wearing a scarf!

All the chapters in Parts II and III include inspirational ideas for reassembling a given room; be sure to check them out. Chapter 2 has a list of helpful finishing tools.

Four Organization Philosophies to Embrace

My organization philosophies in this section are meant to add dimension to the steps you execute when organizing a room. Familiarize yourself with these concepts; if you ever find yourself off-track when you're organizing a room, return to them to refocus your efforts.

Be disciplined

Life runs so much smoother when the members of your household know where to find items and where to return them after use. Drive this point home by sticking to clever systems, locating like items together and putting items away after each use. Here are some suggestions for keeping to a relatively disciplined organization routine:

- ✔ **Set up systems around your home.** Personally, I couldn't run my household without a to-do box and a donate box. Even my kids are onboard! When they've outgrown an item of clothing or toy, they add it to the donate box. When you get a phone call from a charity soliciting donations, say "Yes!" and relish in the fact that your donations are packed and ready to go.

- ✔ **Use baskets, bins, and boxes.** Group like items together, find an appropriate home for them, and label it. Resist the urge to just stuff items in drawers or cabinets. Taking one minute to put items away properly saves many minutes of future frustration associated with trying to find them!

- ✔ **Relax — everyone is allowed to have a junk drawer.** There's probably a drawer in your home that's a constant problem. Nothing in this drawer seems to fit into the other categories, making it an endless source of frustration. Decide to let that drawer be a junk drawer, and move on. Heck, even label it "Junk" if it makes you feel better. As this drawer fills up, weed out the trash, but don't try to make more sense of it. Just be sure to discipline yourself to limit this affliction to a single drawer!

Be green

Reduce, reuse, and recycle! Buy locally. Act globally. Help your neighbor. You're familiar with the earth-friendly catchphrases of the 21st century, but are you living them? Follow these guidelines for keeping your organizational efforts green:

- ✔ **Make green decisions.** You have a choice in every item you purchase or donate. Be green by reducing your purchases, reusing containers you have on hand, and recycling everything you can. If you can, borrow an item instead of buying it.

✔ **Act locally.** Donate gently used items to local women's shelters, charities, and schools. Use your purchasing power to support local businesses and help your chosen neighborhood flourish. A community is built from within, so do your part!

Be frugal

Once it's organized, the best way to maintain your space is to reduce the influx of items coming in. When you're about to buy an item, ask yourself this series of questions: "Do I need it?," "Can I afford it?," "Can I borrow it from someone else?," "Can I get it secondhand?," and "Can I store it?" You may be surprised by your answers! When you do purchase a new item, follow the sage advice of "one in, one out": If you buy that new sweater, prepare to get rid of an old one.

Here are a few additional ideas for embracing your frugal side:

✔ **Repurpose items.** I'm a firm believer in the fact that you can accomplish a lot of organization without spending money. Cardboard boxes and old jars are far better organizational devices than piles of stuff on the floor. Consider turning an old door into a desk, repurposing an unused wine rack as a magazine holder, or transforming an old shower rod into a clothing bar.

✔ **Stop paying for storage.** If you're currently paying for offsite storage, I encourage you to give your 30-day notice. Employing the tips in this book will help you weed through the items in storage and determine if they support the goal for your home. Donating or selling unnecessary items from storage will make you feel better, and the money you save from eliminating this fee goes straight to your bottom line!

✔ **Regift.** You're bound to come across unopened items when sorting through a room. Return things for which you have the receipt, and regift whatever else you can (gifts that were nice but not to your taste, for example).

Be clever

When you see a chance to make life easier, go for it! In general, start with less stuff to manage and fewer things to do, and you'll soon find that you have fewer frustrations in life. Remember, when it comes to stuff, less is more! Consider these guidelines:

✔ **Imitation is the most sincere form of flattery.** There's a reason that home organization stores, magazines, and TV shows are so inspirational — they display the work of professionals! If you see an idea you love, copy it!

✔ **Less is more.** Purchase toys that don't require batteries, which need frequent changing. Cancel subscriptions for magazines you don't have time to read. Get rid of items you use less than once a year and struggle to store. Small changes like these add up and result in more time, less frustration, and fewer items on your to-do list!

✔ **Embrace technology.** Store your DVDs and CDs in media folders. Upload your CDs to your hard drive. Scan your photos onto your computer. Embrace technology whenever you can, but don't forget to back up your hard drive regularly.

Chapter 2

The Tools and Time You Need

Tell your personal trainer you're taking some time off — because home organization is an excellent workout! Expect to work up a sweat by sorting items, installing projects, and putting the finishing touches on rooms in your home. This chapter provides you with detailed information on the tools needed to whip your house into shape. They're divided into three categories: sorting tools, installation tools, and finishing tools. Additionally, I fill you in on the details of my handy do-it-yourself kit, which is a great stocked caddy to carry room to room when organizing. (Flip to Chapter 3 for specifics on using all these tools.)

In this chapter, I also help you develop a time frame for organizing rooms. This estimate includes planning and sorting time as well as time for shopping, installing projects, and reassembling a room. You'll want to give your personal trainer an estimate of when you'll be back to the gym, right?

Gathering Your Tools

Save valuable running around time by gathering the tools in the following sections before you start a project. When you're inspired and on a roll, you don't want to break your momentum and run to the hardware store to buy a plastic bin or a level.

Sorting tools

Roll up your sleeves and get to it! The easiest way to make sense of a room is to remove all the stuff, sort it, and put it all back in a logical manner (see Chapter 1 for an introduction to sorting). Sorting is a fast-paced task, and you can stay on top of the game by having a supply of simple sorting tools on hand (see Figure 2-1). You'll use these items for tackling each room:

  ✔ **Bins:** Use large, sturdy plastic containers. I recommend getting high-quality jumbo bins (at least 65 gallons) because they need to hold a lot of weight!

✔ **Neon construction paper and markers:** Purchase paper in four different colors (like neon yellow, green, orange, and pink) to correspond to the four sorting categories. Label the signs with large block letters: STAY, MOVE, SHARE, and GO. When you're working quickly and efficiently, a large, clearly marked sign catches your eye and helps you hit the right target from 20 feet across the room. (You want your old shoe to end up in SHARE, not STAY!)

✔ **Trash bags:** When you find your sorting groove, your bins are likely to fill up fast. Have a supply of sturdy large trash bags on hand to periodically empty out your SHARE and GO bins in particular. Label your trash bags (so your SHARE pile doesn't end up in the trash), and get back to sorting!

Figure 2-1: An assortment of sorting tools.

Installation tools

The projects in this book are simple, straightforward, and use many of the same tools again and again. For example, in almost every project, you need a pencil, stud finder, screwdriver, and level. You probably already have them in your garage! Some of the more advanced installations require a nail gun and carpenter's square, and — don't be intimidated — you may have to work from the top of a ladder. Here are the most commonly used installation tools in this book (see Figure 2-2):

✔ **Everyday tools:** Phillips screwdriver, flathead screwdriver, hammer, and pencil

✔ **Power tools:** Drill, drill bits, nail gun, and safety goggles

✔ **Carpentry items:** Level, carpenter's square, measuring tape, ladder, stud finder, nails, screws, and drywall anchors

Don't forget painting supplies! You've decluttered your space and have a plan for projects and furniture rearrangements, but something still isn't right! Before you return all your STAY items to a room, celebrate your newly organized space with a coat (or two) of paint in a new color. Try zesty red, fuchsia, or turquoise for an energizing effect; aqua, sage, or gray for a calming effect; or cream, navy, or beige for a traditional feel. You've earned it!

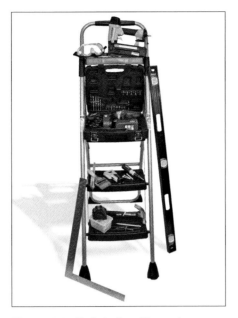

Figure 2-2: Tools for installing projects.

Finishing tools

A room isn't complete until it's *finished*. By this, I mean that all items should be put away in containers, clearly labeled and artfully arranged, and all your furniture and accessories should be back in place. If you like the way the revamped room looks, you're more likely to maintain your organized space going forward. Here are a few helpful items for finishing a room (see Figure 2-3):

✔ **Bins, baskets, and boxes:** Good job on the sorting . . . now put it all away. Review your collection of STAY items and decide on the best container for them. A bin? A basket? A box? Select a container with features that make sense for your items. Do you want something with an open top or closed? Clear, opaque, woven, leather, or plastic? The choice is yours!

In Parts II and III, I provide suggestions for containers and other gadgets geared toward specific rooms. Be sure to check them out.

✔ **Label maker:** Reinforce your hard work by labeling your bins, baskets, and boxes. The visual cues will help you commit to your organized space, and others will follow your lead. I find it really hard to put a box of pasta on a shelf labeled "Canned foods," don't you?

✔ **Scented candles or scent diffusers:** The final layer of a complete room is scent. (I'm a huge fan of peppermint and lavender.) Scent can totally transform your mood. Try it!

Your own do-it-yourself kit

Are you committed to organizing your bedroom? Your whole home? Your workplace? If you see do-it-yourself organizing in your future, treat yourself to a kit that holds your tools and sources of inspiration. Think of it as your briefcase!

Figure 2-3: A few finishing touches for an organized room.

Select a box that's sturdy, roomy, and easy to carry around. I recommend a size somewhere between a makeup case and a standard toolbox. Fill your do-it-yourself kit with the following items (see Figure 2-4):

- ✔ **Tools:** Label maker, labels, screwdrivers, screws, small hammer, nails, stud finder, small level, measuring tape, pencil, marker, and a small pad of paper

- ✔ **Inspiration:** Color wheel, paint swatches, inspirational photos from magazines, and home organization catalogs

 I store my do-it-yourself kit in my office because it's centrally located in my home. If I'm inspired by a project or tip I see online or in a magazine, I can just grab my kit and take it with me room to room. Given that the kit is visible in the room, I wanted to select a box that's attractive and coordinates with the décor of my home office. My kit is silver; what color inspires you?

Figure 2-4: A handy do-it-yourself kit loaded with organizing essentials.

Estimating Your Organizing Time

This book arms you with inspirational tips and clever projects. As you read through them, I expect the little voice in the back of your head to chime in, saying "How long is this going to take?" Whether you do only one project in a room or organize an entire room from scratch, you need to develop a game plan for what you want to do in the space, sorting the contents, shopping for supplies, putting together the projects, and reassembling the space. In the following sections, I break down the amount of time you need to organize a room and provide an easy plan for a weekend session.

Each project in this book has an accompanying time frame, such as "less than an hour" or "less than half a day," so you have a good idea of how long it takes to finish a particular project.

Breaking down the amount of time needed to organize an entire room

You may look at Parts II and III and choose only a handful of projects for a room, but what if you want to overhaul an entire space? The following guidelines give you an idea of how many work hours you may need to organize different size spaces from start to finish. Keep in mind this is just an estimate and everyone works at his or her own pace!

- **Large space room organization:** Kitchen (Chapter 5), bedroom/closet (Chapter 6), home office (Chapter 8), or garage (Chapter 11)
  - **Breakdown:** Planning (1–2 hours), sorting (2–3 hours), shopping (1–2 hours), building projects (2–4 hours), and reassembling the room (2–4 hours)
  - **Total:** Up to 15 hours (allow 20 if you plan to paint)
- **Medium space room organization:** Entryway/living room (Chapter 4) or kids' space (Chapter 9)
  - **Breakdown:** Planning (0–1 hour), sorting (1–2 hours), shopping (1–2 hours), building projects (1–3 hours), and reassembling the room (1–2 hours)
  - **Total:** Up to 10 hours (allow 15 if you plan to paint)
- **Small space room organization:** Bathroom (Chapter 7) or laundry (Chapter 10)
  - **Breakdown:** Planning (0–1 hour), sorting (0–1 hour), shopping (1–2 hours), building projects (1–2 hours), and reassembling the room (0–1 hour)
  - **Total:** Up to 7 hours (allow 12 if you plan to paint)

The preceding list illustrates that with a little hard work and caffeine, you can transform any room in your house in under 24 work hours.

Outlining a plan for weekend warriors

If your daily routine involves working 9 to 5 (or similar hours), the weekend is probably the best time for you to tackle projects. By planning ahead and sticking to the following schedule, you can complete an entire room in a weekend!

1. **During the week**

   Read the appropriate chapter of this book, and ponder what projects are right for your space. Cancel any weekend engagements so that you can work uninterrupted and without distractions.

2. **Friday evening**

   Unplug your telephone. Grab a buddy, and empty the entire contents of the room, sorting as you go into bins labeled STAY, MOVE, SHARE, and GO. Play upbeat music and sip caffeinated beverages to make the process go faster! (1–4 hours)

   Review the STAY box to determine what will stay in the room, and fine-tune the projects you plan to build or install. Record any measurements necessary to build your projects, such as the height of your pantry, the amount of space available inside a kitchen cabinet, or the dimensions of your closet. (1–2 hours)

   Compile your shopping list, which should include tools, materials, paint, lumber, and so on. Double-check your measurements and project list to be sure that you get the right items in the correct sizes on your first shopping trip! (30 minutes)

   Get a good night's sleep!

3. **Saturday**

   Early morning: Prep your walls, and apply the first coat of paint. (1–2 hours)

   Late morning: While the first coat of paint dries, hit the home improvement store to buy all the items on your list. (2 hours)

   Midday: Return home and get started on building and installing your projects. Install anything that doesn't interfere with painting the walls, such as closet organizers. (4 hours)

   Late afternoon: Add the second coat of paint (1–2 hours) before you hit the sack.

   If you don't plan to paint the room, you can start grouping like items in containers and labeling them. If your adrenaline is still pumping, you can bag up all the items you plan to donate and move them to your garage. Don't forget to itemize donations for your tax write-off!

4. **Sunday**

   In the morning, move your furniture back into the room and fine-tune your furniture arrangement. Install any remaining projects. (1–2 hours)

   Return your STAY items to the room, methodically selecting the proper bin, basket, or box to contain everything, labeling them, and artfully arranging them. (2–4 hours)

Approaching a room organization project with the help of a team is a great way to showcase every member's strengths! Develop a firm game plan in which everyone has a job. For example, your energetic teen can empty the room while your spouse applies a new coat of paint, your contractor neighbor gets to work installing a wall cabinet, and you shop for bins, baskets, and boxes. Just make sure your team has a captain, and everyone knows who it is . . . a clipboard and a megaphone should do the trick.

Chapter 3
Nailing Down Carpentry Fundamentals

Home organization involves lots of emptying and sorting because you have to pare down the contents of a space before you can reassemble your room. After you empty and sort a room, the real fun begins — building projects! This chapter familiarizes you with basic carpentry techniques and frequently asked questions. There's no need to be intimidated by carpentry; all the projects in this book are simple enough for the average homeowner to complete.

Hammering Out Basic Carpentry Techniques

Quality techniques ensure quality finished products. Just about every project in this book instructs you to measure dimensions, locate a wall stud or ceiling joist, and use tools. This section provides specific instructions on these basic carpentry techniques.

Measuring length, width, and height

Accurate projects begin with accurate measurements, hence the expression "measure twice, cut once." This approach works infinitely better than measuring, cutting, repurchasing the item, measuring again, and cutting again.

Measurements are usually taken and listed in order of length, width, and then height. If you're not sure which measurement is length and which is width, length is the longer of the two (if there's a difference). Height references how tall an item is, and depth also may be used in place of width, depending on what you're measuring.

When taking any measurement, measure the distance in at least three places and use the smallest number. For example, measure the width of a wall nook along the back wall, halfway between the back wall and the opening, and at the edge of the opening. Use the smallest number as your final width measurement to make sure that whatever you're planning to put in the nook will fit properly.

Locating a wall stud or ceiling joist

The walls of most homes consist of sheets of drywall nailed or screwed into vertical wood framing. *Studs* are the vertical, 1½-inch thick 2-x-4-inch pieces of wood framing. Studs are generally located every 16 inches, and you have to find and use them when hanging heavy items on the wall. Installing heavy items in drywall only is unsafe, even if you use drywall anchors (see the later section "When do you use drywall anchors?"). Ceiling joists are the same as wall studs except that they run across the ceiling instead of vertically down the walls.

You can go about locating a wall stud or a ceiling joist in one of several ways (if you're looking for a joist, grab a ladder!).

- ✔ **The right tool for the job:** A *stud finder* detects the nails or screws used to attach drywall to studs. Just hold the finder to the wall or ceiling and run it slowly along the length of the wall or across the ceiling; when the device detects a nail or screw — and therefore the stud — it beeps or lights up.

- ✔ **The good old knocking method:** Hollow walls sound very different from dense wood. Walk along a wall and knock the wall with your knuckles as you go. The hollow (drywall) portion will sound very flat, and the stud (wood) portion will sound very sharp.

- ✔ **The outlet technique:** Wall outlets are installed in wall studs, so you can assume that there's a wall stud within 1 inch or so of every wall outlet. Use your stud finder or trusty knuckle to verify.

- ✔ **The magnet test:** If you're leery of the results of your stud finder or knuckles, you can find a stud with a magnet. Select the wall area where you intend to hang your item and slowly move a magnet in a snaking pattern along this wall. When your magnet crosses a nail or screw in the drywall and stud, it sticks to the metal, and you know you've found a stud!

Using a level

A *level,* also called a *carpenter's level, spirit level,* or *bubble level,* indicates whether marks or an installation are perfectly level (horizontal) or plumb (vertical). The level is a rectangular device with a number of glass tubes each containing liquid with an air bubble. If you hold the level against the object you're checking and the bubble is centered within its marked guide on the glass tube, the object is level or plumb; if the bubble is off to one side, you need to readjust the item and check for level or plumb again.

Using a square

A *square,* also called a *carpenter's square* or a *framing square,* indicates whether an installation is at a perfect right angle (90-degree angle). The square has one long arm and one short arm and is made of aluminum or steel. A square can determine in a single measurement if two items are at a right angle, whereas using a level for that purpose requires a series of horizontal and vertical measurements. To check a right angle, position one end of the square along the adjacent wall or ceiling and the other along the item that you're hanging (see Figure 3-1).

Figure 3-1: A square checks that items (such as holes for drilling) are at a right angle to an adjacent wall, surface, or straight edge.

You also can use a square to establish that two items, like shelves, are parallel. To do so, place one end of the square along the vertical edge of one shelf and the other end of the square along the horizontal edge of a second object.

Using a screwdriver

The two main types of screwdrivers are Phillips and flathead:

- **Phillips screwdrivers** install screws with an X on the head. Most manufactured products — like message boards, medicine cabinets, and floating shelving — include mounting hardware with these types of screws. Phillips screwdrivers allow the user to get a two-way grip between the screwdriver and the screw and install the item without any side-to-side slipping.

- **Flathead screwdrivers** install screws with a straight slot on the head. Specialty screws and the screws that hold outlet covers usually have flathead screws. You can also use your flathead screwdriver for opening paint cans.

To install any screw, select a screwdriver with the right head and handle length to accommodate your project. Twist in a clockwise (to the right) direction. To remove the screw, twist in a counterclockwise (to the left) direction. (Don't forget: "Righty tighty, lefty loosey.")

Using an electric drill

An electric drill is a power tool that can drill a hole through almost anything! Before drilling, you need to select the proper type of drill bit (different bits are designed to drill through wood, masonry, metal, glass, and so on) and size of drill bit (¼ inch, ⅜ inch, ½ inch, ⅝ inch, and so on). For a strong installation, always use a drill bit that's slightly smaller than the screw being inserted into the hole. Here's where math comes in handy! If you're going to install a ½-inch screw, recall that ½ equals ⅜ or ⁹⁄₁₆, and so you should use a slightly smaller bit like a ⅜ inch or ⁷⁄₁₆ inch. If you drill a hole that's the same size or larger than the screw, the installation won't be as strong as with a smaller hole because the screw will be loose in the hole.

In this book, you use an electric drill only to drill holes, not to insert screws. When you use an electric drill to insert screws, the drill tends to wobble and enlarge the opening of the hole, which reduces the strength of the hold.

Prepare for your installation by marking the spot you intend to drill into and ensuring you can drill at a perpendicular angle by using a ladder or crouching down. If you have to reach above your head to drill, the hole is likely to slant upward, lessening the strength of your installation. After selecting the proper drill bit for your installation, make sure your drill is in "Forward" mode and apply consistent horizontal pressure to the marked spot as you pull the trigger, as shown in Figure 3-2. (Of course, if you're drilling into the ceiling, you apply consistent vertical pressure.) You should feel some resistance after about ½ inch as your drill passes through the drywall and enters the wood stud (I discuss studs earlier in this chapter). When your drill bit is completely into the wood and you can't drill any farther, pull your drill out of the stud or switch your drill into "Reverse" mode, and the drill bit should easily retract.

Figure 3-2: Drill your holes perpendicular to a wall by starting off at the right height.

Answering a Few Frequently Asked Carpentry Questions

Carpentry, like any field, has its share of frequently asked questions. This section provides insight into commonly encountered carpentry situations.

Should you use wood board or plywood for your project?

When you understand the difference between different types of wood products, it's easier to decide which one is appropriate for your project. Here's the breakdown:

✔ **Wood board** is a solid piece of wood cut from the vertical length of a tree. It's available in either softwood (fir, pine, cedar) or hardwood (oak); hardwood is considerably more expensive than softwood. Wood board is great for projects in which the wood is visible, like a shelf with visible wood grain. If you plan to paint your project, you can use less expensive plywood.

Visible knots and disfigurations can mar the appearance, and subsequently reduce the price, of wood lumber. Some people appreciate the natural look of real lumber, though, so if you choose to use wood board for your project, you may want to show it off by applying a wood stain or veneer.

Wood board comes in several standard sizes, like 1x4. This size is misleading, though; the dimensions of a 1x4 are really ¾ x 3½ inches. The standard sizes refer to the thickness of a rough cut of raw lumber, but some wood (¼ to ½ inch) is inevitably lost when the lumber is milled to create the final cut.

✔ **Plywood** is constructed of many thin layers of wood glued together, and it's less expensive than wood board. The way that the layers are glued together — with the grains going in opposite directions — makes plywood very strong, so it's good to use when you need to drill through the thickness of the wood or when you need a large sheet of wood for the back of a cabinet or the base of a box. The top of plywood is attractive when sanded and stained, but the edge will never be as attractive as wood board because you can see all the glued-together layers. Plywood comes in several standard thicknesses, such as ⅛ inch, ¼ inch, ⅜ inch, and so on. Plywood sheets come in one standard size, 48x96, but your local store may carry additional cuts.

Can you use nails rather than screws?

I advocate a screw and screwdriver installation over a hammer and nail installation throughout this book because . . . well, screws are better. Screws are stronger because they grip the wood as they're inserted, you can install them perfectly straight if you predrill your holes with a drill, and you can uninstall and reinstall screws without damage. If there's a chance that you'll remove your item from the wall or wherever it's installed, you should always use screws.

Don't throw away your hammer (or nail gun) just yet, though! Nails are recommended if you're trying to install a fastener into the thickness of plywood because a drill and screw installation may split the wood. An example of this installation is nailing through one piece of wood into another to form a corner of a wood box. You also can use nails if you can't maneuver an electric drill into a tight spot, like a drawer or the inside of a cabinet (see the next section for details).

The advantage of using nails rather than screws in some situations is that installation is much faster! You don't need to predrill holes, and you can drive in nails in seconds. You also can hide nails by using a nail set to drive the nail farther into the wood, and covering the nail head with wood putty. Just make sure it's a permanent installation before burying the nail head with a nail set!

What if your drill won't fit into tight spaces?

Some projects require you to drill holes in tight spaces, like the cabinet under the sink. If you can't maneuver your drill in this area, try using a hammer and nail to create a hole for your screw. Use a nail with a diameter that's slightly smaller than the diameter of the screw to ensure a tight fit. After you tap in the nail partway, use the claw side of the hammer to remove the nail. You have a hole ready for your screw!

When do you use drywall anchors?

Often the only thing supporting the weight of an object hanging on a wall is a single screw drilled into a stud. But what if a stud isn't available? Drilling the screw directly into drywall only is a recipe for disaster. When there's no wood stud where you need to hang an item, turn to drywall anchors. *Drywall anchors* are plastic or metal inserts that fit into holes drilled in drywall and then accept the mounting screws; an anchor can strengthen the installation of a screw into drywall by expanding and trapping the screw in the wall. An installation using drywall anchors isn't as reliable as screwing into a stud, but it's better than using a plain screw in drywall.

Most products include drywall anchors as part of the mounting materials. Drywall anchors come in standard sizes that correspond to the standard sizes of screws; for example, a ³⁄₁₆-inch diameter screw requires an anchor with an internal ³⁄₁₆-inch diameter. The anchor wraps around the screw, and you need to use a larger drill bit (slightly smaller than the size of the external diameter of the anchor) to install the anchor.

Different anchors are available, depending on the weight of the item you're hanging:

✔ For lightweight items like decorations and small wall shelves, use plastic or metal wall anchors. Drill a hole into the wall that's slightly smaller than the anchor. Insert the anchor by hand, and tap it with your hammer until it goes all the way into the hole. Install your screw into the anchor using a screwdriver.

✔ For heavier items like large picture frames, mirrors, and sturdy shelves, you need to use a stronger fixture like a Molly bolt or toggle bolt. These items spring open when they're installed through the drywall, and they widen the grip of the screw. Insert Molly bolts or toggle bolts by drilling a hole wide enough for the bolt to fit through, inserting the bolt, and triggering it open by turning the screw clockwise with your screwdriver (see Figure 3-3). When the bolt is open, you'll feel resistance because the fixture has fully opened against the drywall. Sometimes you need a second screwdriver to do this.

Figure 3-3: Screwing into a drywall anchor for a heavy fixture.

Part II
Organizing Primary Spaces in Your Home

"We're trying to get the music room as organized as the kitchen."

In this part . . .

This part of the book is devoted to organizing the major workhorses of your home — your entryway/living room, kitchen, bedroom/closet, bathroom, and home office. These are the primary living spaces in your home, and with each subsequent transformation, your home life will run smoother. An organized space promotes an organized life, and before long you and your family will be performing day-to-day tasks quicker and more efficiently. Isn't this what you've been waiting for?

Each chapter in this part focuses entirely on one key space in your house, and I walk you through organizing the room start to finish. I help you identify the goal of the space, address the room's limitations, empty and sort the contents, build projects, and complete the room with finishing touches. Experience the transformation from a frustrating cluttered space that makes you anxious to a peaceful room with everything in its place. Blissful bedrooms, clutter-free kitchens, and more await you.

Chapter 4

First Impressions: Streamlining Your Entryway and Living Room

Tasks performed in this chapter

- ✔ Hanging a sturdy peg rack
- ✔ Converting entryway space into a storage area
- ✔ Creating a custom magazine rack in your living room

The function and goal of the entryway and living room is to graciously welcome you into a warm, inviting space while simultaneously gathering and storing your purse, hat, coat, gloves, and scarf. This is the space guests see first as they walk through the front door, and people will develop a first impression of the way you live based on this space. A pile of clothing and accessories on the floor signals a household that's disorganized and careless, whereas a streamlined and visually interesting space showcases your strengths. Because perception is key, put your best foot forward! Your goal is to transform your entryway and living room into a visually appealing space that stores a deceptive amount of clothing, accessories, media, and literature.

Most homes don't have a large, formal entryway with room for a fancy console table, a dramatic chandelier, and stunning artwork and accessories. Generally, an entryway is just the initial passageway between the front door and the living room. If you have a few feet of available wall space, you can convert this passageway into an effective flytrap that captures coats, purses, and hats as people come through the front door. If your family uses an entryway/mudroom that attaches to your garage or back door, you can still use the projects and tips in this chapter to enhance your storage in that area.

When you organize your entryway and living room, you have to work around the limitations that are specific to your space. Identify your limitations by answering these questions:

- ✔ Do you watch TV or listen to music in your living room? If so, do you have enough storage for CDs, DVDs, remote controls, and video games?

- ✔ Do you have a desk or computer in your living room?

- ✔ Is your home library in your living room? Do you have enough storage for your books?

- ✔ Do you need to dress up your fireplace mantle or foyer table?

- ✔ Are you displaying too many decorations and knickknacks?

After you address the goals and limitations of your entryway and living room, it's time to review their contents. Each item should fall into one of the following four categories:

✔ **STAY:** This item is in good condition, is used often, is relevant to the goal, and will stay in the room. Examples are entryway items (frequently used coats, scarves, hats, backpacks, sunglasses, umbrellas, and shoes), furniture (couches, tables, lamps, and pet beds), tasteful accessories, media components, board games, books, and photo albums.

✔ **MOVE:** This item is in good condition and is used often, but it doesn't belong in the entryway or living room. Examples are pet supplies, exercise equipment, and work projects.

✔ **SHARE:** This item is in good condition but hasn't been used in the last year, is a duplicate, or no longer serves the goal of the space. Examples are unnecessary or outdated furniture, media components, board games, books, and unused photo albums.

✔ **GO:** These broken or damaged items are trash!

After you determine what stays in your entryway and living room, select the projects in this chapter that will help you maximize the storage in this space. When you're done, check out the section "The Finishing Touches: Reassembling Your Entryway and Living Room" at the end of this chapter for ideas on maintaining your room's organization.

Decorating the designer way

By adding a few decorative shelves and sprucing up your entryway's foyer table and living room's fireplace mantle, you can turn your ordinary house into an exquisite home. Trim back your decorations and accessories to those that are consistent with the décor of your home and in good condition — and that you like looking at! Large, solid-colored items tend to read better visually than small knickknacks. Keep a room interesting by changing out your accents with each season!

Your foyer table is an excellent place to make a quality first impression. It's more decorative than functional, so focus on showcasing framed photos or fresh flowers. Large items like lamps or floral displays look best individually, whereas smaller items like candles look best in groups of three. The coffee table is best left empty or adorned with a single decoration or a stack of books — leave room for the coffee!

Here are some tips for your mantle:

✔ Empty it of any clutter and media or electronics paraphernalia. The mantle is an architectural feature that deserves to be shown off!

✔ Dress up your empty mantle with candles, picture frames, and vases in colors that accent your living room décor.

✔ Rather than redecorating your entire room for each holiday, consider concentrating your holiday décor on your mantle. Potted flowers and pastel eggs signal the beginning of spring. A collection of gourds and colorful leaves make an interesting fall display, and you probably have some prized Christmas or other holiday items that deserve top billing on the mantle.

✔ If you don't have a mantle, install a wood shelf or beam above your fireplace, and then decorate it as you would a mantle. (Check out Chapter 7 for basic instructions on installing whimsical wall shelves.)

Hanging an Entryway Peg Rack

"May I take your coat?" Offering to take a guest's coat is a thoughtful gesture . . . if you have a suitable place to store it. If you want to hang coats and purses in your entryway but don't have a roomy coat closet, try a wall-mounted peg rack! These racks are designed to hold a substantial amount of weight on individual pegs and are a great alternative to clumsy, wobbly coat racks. Select a sturdy model with a wood tone or paint color that blends in with the wall it will be mounted on; after all, this item is more functional than decorative. Many models have double hooks in lieu of pegs that allow you to store both a coat and a hat on an individual hook. Isn't that clever?

A peg rack needs to be installed into one or more wall studs.

Identify the location of your peg rack. If your entryway door opens to the left, consider the adjacent wall on the left side of the door so the door will naturally disguise the peg rack when ajar. Select a height that accommodates all members of your family (usually around 50 to 60 inches so that coats won't drag on the floor), and mark the height on the wall.

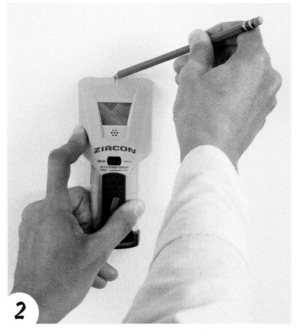

Locate and mark two or three wall studs at your desired height with a stud finder. Sturdy peg racks that support the weight of heavy coats need to be installed into one or more wall studs, and the number of studs you use depends on the width of your rack.

Hold the rack to the wall along the studs at your chosen height and use a pencil to mark through the holes where you'll drill. Note that some models require that you detach the hanging mechanisms from the rack before you hang it.

Use a level to ensure that the hole marks from Step 3 are even.

5

Using a drill bit that's slightly smaller than the screws required to hang the rack, drill holes in the marked spots, applying consistent horizontal pressure.

7

Screw the rack into the wall with a screwdriver.

6

If any of holes you drilled in Step 5 aren't installed into wall studs, insert drywall anchors to strengthen the installation. Drill holes that are slightly smaller than the anchors, tap the anchors into the holes with a hammer, and insert the screws.

TIP

If you have small children in your household, you can tuck a small step stool in this area to enable them to access the rack.

Converting Entryway Space into a Storage Area

A nook (or any space) near an entryway is an ideal candidate for shoe storage, hanging storage, and accessory storage, all in one convenient location. Before purchasing your storage components, accurately measure the dimensions of your space. Measure the height along the back wall. Determine the depth by measuring from the front to the back of the space, and determine the width by measuring from the left side wall to the right side.

Write down your measurements, and then carefully plan your components. A storage tower is comprised of a lower level slotted shoe rack or storage bench for shoes, a mid-level locker/cabinet for coats or backpacks, and an overhead cubby for purses, wallets, keys, and other small items. Shop for tower components with a similar width because they'll be stacked vertically, and make sure you have enough width and depth in your space for all the components you buy. Also make sure that you have enough height for each tower. If you're running into height constraints, I recommend using a shoe rack instead of a storage bench.

1

Locate the wall studs in the back of your space with a stud finder and mark them in pencil.

2

Determine the height of the locker by measuring the distance from the bottom to the top of the locker.

3

To determine the height at which to hang the locker, add together the height of the shoe storage (with lid open, if using a bench) and the measurement from Step 2. Measure the total distance from the floor along the wall stud and mark it in pencil.

Note that nooks often have a front wall overhang that defines the space. This means that you can store items up to the full ceiling height of the nook along the back wall, but the front wall overhang may make stowing and retrieving items difficult. Make sure that the front wall overhang of the nook (if there is one) doesn't interfere with retrieving items from the upper cubby.

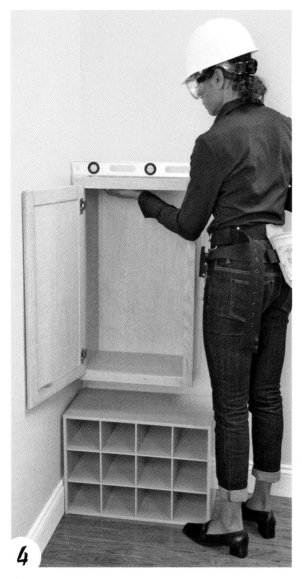

4

Align the top of the locker with the height you marked in Step 3. Use a level to ensure that your locker will hang evenly.

5

With a helper holding the locker in place and using a drill bit that's slightly smaller than the screws required for the installation, drill holes through the back of the locker and into the wall studs, applying consistent horizontal pressure.

If you have the space, consider building a storage tower for each member of your household. If you have a very large household or limited space, members can share storage.

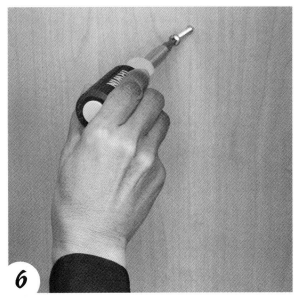

6 Screw the locker into the wall with a screwdriver.

8 Using a drill bit that's slightly smaller than the screw required for the installation, drill holes in the marked spots, using consistent horizontal pressure. (If the holes don't line up with the wall studs marked in Step 1, add drywall anchors to strengthen the installation.)

7 Center the cubby on top of the locker, and use a pencil to mark holes for drilling through the hanging mechanisms.

9 With a helper holding the cubby in place, screw the cubby into the wall with a screwdriver.

10 Repeat this installation for additional storage towers.

You can transform *any* space or nook in your home into prime storage for grab-and-go storage, not just areas in your entryway.

Building a Living Room Magazine Rack

Stuff You Need to Know

Toolbox:
- Dropcloths or newspaper
- Medium-grit sandpaper
- Clean rags
- Stir stick
- Paintbrush or sponge brush
- Pencil
- Measuring tape
- Drill
- $\frac{5}{16}$-inch drill bit
- Safety goggles
- Level
- Nail gun
- 3-inch nails

Materials:
- $\frac{1}{4}$-inch dowels cut to 17 inches in length
- Two 1x2 hardwood boards
- Paint or wood stain
- End caps for dowels (plastic or metal)

Time Needed:
Less than half a day

Subscribing to four magazines a year (like the average American household) and saving all your back issues adds up to about 24 horizontal inches of storage a year. People tend to forget that magazines are meant to be enjoyed and recycled!

This project is a clever solution for storing the *current* issues of your favorite magazines. This magazine rack has several rows of hanging space to display (and mark your spot in) the magazines you're *actively* reading. The rack consists of narrow vertical wood beams that support horizontal "magazine holder" dowels; you insert the dowels into drilled holes in the beams.

You need one dowel per magazine, so purchase the desired number of $\frac{1}{4}$-inch wooden dowels at your local hardware store and have them cut into 17-inch lengths. Purchase two hardwood 1x2 side supports that will attach to the wall and support the dowels (see Chapter 3 for more information on lumber). The length of the rails depends on the number of dowels on your rack; allow 10 inches per dowel. For example, for a five-dowel rack, you need two 50-inch 1x2s.

1 Prepare a well-ventilated painting area (like a garage with the door open) by laying down dropcloths or newspaper to protect the workspace.

2

Lightly sand the wooden dowels and supports, and then wipe them down with a clean, damp rag to prepare the surface for paint or stain.

3

Use a stir stick to stir the paint or stain you plan to use on the dowels and supports to match them to the décor of your living room. Use a paintbrush or sponge brush to apply the product to the dowels and supports according to the manufacturer's directions.

Note: Let the paint or stain dry completely before you move on to Step 4.

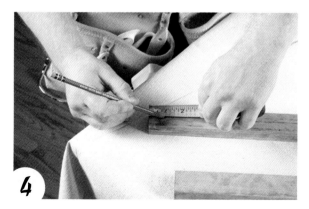

4

Using a pencil, measure and mark your first spot to drill 1 inch from the end of one support. Be sure to mark the 2-inch side of the 1x2.

5

Mark 10-inch increments on the support, starting with the mark from Step 4. Repeat the measuring and marking on the second support.

6 Position one wood support on a surface that you can drill completely through to, whether it's a workbench, sawhorse, or even on grass in your yard. Hold the support firmly in place, and use a ⁵⁄₁₆-inch drill bit to drill all the way through the wood support at your first mark 1 inch from the end, applying consistent vertical pressure. Continue to drill all remaining holes on both supports.

7 Decide where to hang your magazine rack in your living room, and locate a wall stud with a stud finder. Mark along the stud in pencil.

8 Position the 1-inch side of your first side support vertically along the wall stud. Use a level to ensure that the side support is completely vertical. (You may want to have a helper hold the support in place while you prepare to attach it to the wall.)

9 Wearing safety goggles, use a nail gun loaded with 3-inch nails to nail through the 1-inch side of the 1x2 and into the wall. Continue nailing the first support to the wall, making sure to locate nails between the holes for the dowels, every 3 to 4 inches.

If you use dowels with a larger diameter (envision a rolling pin), magazines will slide right off, so ¼ inch is best.

10

Locate a second stud 16 inches from the first wall stud, and mark along the stud in pencil.

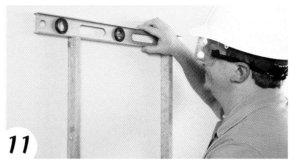

11

Position the 1-inch side of your second side support vertically along this wall stud. Use a level to ensure that the second side support is both completely plumb and level with the first support. (You may want to have a helper hold the support in place while you prepare to attach it to the wall.)

12

Wearing safety goggles, use a nail gun loaded with 3-inch nails to nail through the 1-inch side of the 1x2 and into the wall. Continue nailing the second support to the wall, making sure to locate nails between the holes for the dowels, every 3 to 4 inches.

13

Thread your dowels through each set of holes.

14

Attach end caps to each dowel to prevent it from slipping out.

TIP

How many magazines would you like to display? Three to six is reasonable; if you try to display a dozen magazines on your wall space, your home will start to resemble a waiting room at a dentist's office!

The Finishing Touches: Reassembling Your Entryway and Living Room

After you've installed one, some, or all the projects that appear earlier in this chapter, it's time to put your entryway and living room back together again. The following sections provide some inspirational and functional ideas for continuing to "wow" beyond the first impression.

Organizing furniture and major electronics

You may live in an electronic world, but that doesn't mean you want to look at electronic gadgets and gizmos all the time! Where possible, put the following ideas to use in your home:

- Group your furniture in such a way that the TV isn't the main focal point of the room. For example, highlight your fireplace by angling couches and arm chairs toward this feature. Similarly, you can highlight a picturesque window view with furniture placement.

- Consider transferring your TV to an armoire with doors. You can hide the TV behind closed doors when it isn't in use and enjoy looking at a nice piece of furniture instead of a blank screen.

- Hang a wall of heavy draperies to disguise your flat panel TV. This technique provides an opportunity to add an interesting decorative feature to the room with patterned or solid-colored drapery fabric. Achieve this dramatic effect by hanging draperies just below the ceiling or crown molding. You'll likely need to purchase a custom-sized rod or use a succession of rods to accommodate the full length of the wall.

- If your home office is in your living room, position a folding screen or large potted plant in front of your office nook. This trick visually separates your office space from your living space. (See Chapter 8 for details on organizing your home office.)

Storing movies

Stacks of movies can be frustrating to manage. If you don't have enough room to keep them in a cabinet or container of some sort, the piles collect dust, get knocked over, and are perpetually disorganized so that it's hard to find the movie you want. Most people hold on to movies that they may watch . . . someday. With so many new releases, how can you keep up? Review your collection during the sorting phase I describe at the beginning of this chapter, and ask yourself the following questions:

- Is it a family favorite that you plan to watch again? If the answer is yes, it can stay — for now.

- Have you seen it before and feel you can pass it on? If the answer is yes, move it to your SHARE pile.

✔ Is it a bulky VHS tape? If the answer is yes, consider replacing it with a DVD version. VHS players have almost exclusively been replaced by DVD players (hint, hint). VHS tapes have a shorter lifespan than DVDs and are more difficult to store (hint, hint). If you have a VHS tape with sentimental content, like a wedding or family holiday video, consider having it professionally transferred to a DVD at your local audio/video store or through a number of online options like www.dvdyourmemories.com.

After you've trimmed your movie collection, consider transferring your DVD collection to a media storage folder. About 2 inches wide, the folder unzips to reveal more than 200 DVDs, looks attractive, and is simple to store on a shelf near your DVD player, in a decorative box, or tucked into storage/seating cubes. Recycle the left-over plastic DVD cases and paper inserts.

Music to your ears: Dealing with CDs

Music-lovers or not, most people collect music CDs. Before long, your collection of music can become a wobbly 6-foot tall tower. Then how are you supposed to access that classic ZZ Top disc down at the bottom?

After you sort through your CD collection, donate anything that you won't listen to again and pitch anything that's broken or badly scratched (as I describe at the beginning of this chapter). Consider transferring your remaining music CDs to your computer hard drive. As a backup, you can store your CD collection in a tidy media storage folder on a bookshelf, in a media cabinet, or in a decorative box. Recycle the empty plastic jewel cases and paper inserts.

The plastic sleeves in media storage folders are roomy enough to store the paper inserts that include the album covers and lyrics. If you like the look and feel of these inserts and can't bear to part with the information they contain, store them in the plastic pockets in your media storage folder!

Recent advances in digital technology have made the average person as capable as a music DJ when it comes to storing and accessing music collections. Embrace this revolution, but don't let it take over your space. If you're a music lover, purchase and download music online.

If you prefer to store your CDs in their original jewel cases, there are a multitude of options available for collections small to large. Units are widely available in home or electronic stores and range from 12-CD wire shelves to 500-CD large wooden cabinets. If you plan to store your music in jewel cases, select a unit that's sturdy, matches your room's décor, and can accommodate your entire collection.

Store only the CDs that you love, and leave a little wiggle room on your shelves for new purchases!

Game on! Arranging video game equipment

Many people enjoy playing video games, but they don't enjoy dealing with all the necessary equipment, including

- Consoles
- Accessories (joysticks, nunchucks, steering wheels, boxing gloves, guitars, and so on)
- Game cartridges and discs

Here are a few ideas for taming the tangle of games, cords, and beeping things:

- **Rolling cart:** Rolling carts come in a variety of materials — wire, stainless steel, and plastic. Because video gaming equipment isn't very heavy, any of these materials are ideal.

  Estimate the number of levels you need; I recommend positioning the console on the top, the accessories in the middle, and the cartridges/discs on the bottom. Purchase a rolling cart with a lip on each tray so items don't slip off. Two-tier carts are sufficient to store a console and cartridges. Three- and four-tier carts are best for dealing with odd-shaped accessories like guitars and steering wheels.

  I recommend leaving the console on the cart and plugging the cord directly into your TV. If you're constantly moving your console to and from the cart, it's likely to get damaged. After using your video game cart, collect excess cord length at the back of the console and secure with a twist tie or clip. Return the cart to a nearby hallway closet, spare bedroom, or space underneath a staircase. If you don't have an alternative storage space, you can conceal the cart and its contents with a customized fabric cover.

- **Wire tower:** The wire tower is an inexpensive option very similar to the tiered rolling cart. It's an ideal fit if you want your gaming equipment to be at arm's length and in plain sight — always. The best location for a tower is directly adjacent to your television because it's part of your living room media.

- **Storage cube:** If you want your gaming console connected at all times and only want to store your games and accessories, consider stashing them in a decorative storage ottoman or cube. When no one is gaming, the top can display a collection of magazines or a decorative throw as well as serve as added seating in your living room.

- **Media storage folder:** Like DVDs and CDs (see the previous sections), you can discreetly store video game discs in media storage folders. Store these folders on a bookshelf, in an entertainment center, or hidden in a storage/seating cube. Don't forget to recycle the cases and inserts!

Jazzing up bookshelves

A small home library is a timeless decorating element that enhances the warmth of any home. If you choose to display books in your living room, stick to traditional approaches such as built-in bookshelves and stand-alone bookcases anchored to walls, but don't forget to interject some whimsy! After you sort, share, and pitch books (as I describe at the beginning of this chapter), try the following tips:

✔ **Group books by topic.** You can dedicate shelves to finance, history, romance, travel, architecture — wherever your interests may lie. Add a small framed photo that correlates to the topic on each shelf.

✔ **Group books by size.** If your bookshelves are at fixed heights (meaning they're not adjustable within the bookcase), group books by size. For each size group, start with the shortest book on the outside edge of the shelf and gradually increase in size toward a focal point or even the center of the room. For example, if a bookshelf is on the left side of a fireplace, angle the books from shortest (left) to tallest (right) so they rise toward the fireplace.

✔ **Group books by color.** Add visual interest by grouping your books by color and then arranging them by size, such as all red- and orange-toned books on one shelf from tallest to shortest and all black and blue-toned books on another shelf from shortest to tallest.

✔ **Corral loose books.** Very thin books or paperback manuals are a challenge to display because they don't like to stand up. Gather all such books into a decorative open-top box and use it as a divider between sets of books on shelves.

✔ **Add bookends or heavy objects every 18 inches or so to prevent slipping.** Heavy ceramic vases, fossils, and beer steins are interesting choices. Use pieces that fit within the decorating scheme of your living room.

✔ **Add unexpected accessories with a personal touch, like old-fashioned cameras, hand-painted coconuts, or small African drums.**

✔ **Display a collection of oversized books on your coffee table.** Select three to five books and stack them with the largest on the bottom. Change your collection regularly.

✔ **Make your bookshelves pop by painting the back wall of the bookcase an accent color that complements other parts of your room.**

If you have a large volume of books in your SHARE pile, consider donating them to your local library or selling them at a used-book store. Or after reading a particularly good book, write a personal note in the front cover and pass it on to a friend or neighbor. To maintain a reasonable collection going forward, stick to the principle of "One in, one out."

Putting together fabulous photo albums

When it comes to photos, less is more. Only keep photographs that feature the subjects looking at the camera (or at least looking good), highlight a memory, or capture those people who are dear to you. Discard boring or unflattering pictures. Duplicate photos can be discarded or shared with friends and family.

Create quality photo albums by highlighting the best parts of an event, vacation, or time period. Select photos for your albums that show a mixture of candid and posed photos, a variety of subjects, and a variety of emotions. For example, reinforce wonderful memories from your cousin's wedding with a page featuring a black-and-white photo of the bride, a group photo with your side of the family, the ring bearer goofing off, and your grandmother giving a heartfelt toast. Now that's a memory!

Sharing photo albums allows you to connect with your friends and family, recall funny memories, and retell old stories. Make the most of this experience by sticking to the following tips:

- **Photo preservation:** Use acid-free albums and photo paper to extend the life of your prints. For photos that you don't place in albums, store them in an archival quality box to protect them from mold, dust, and pests. Store the box in an area of your home that's free of moisture, bright light, and extreme temperatures, such as the top of the entryway closet or in an entertainment center cabinet.

- **Photo albums:** Don't overdo it! Buy a few basic albums and fill them up with a handful of photos per event. For example, label a book "Vacation Memories" and add 10 to 20 photos per trip. People looking through your album would rather see the highlights of a few family trips than the play-by-play of one single trip.

- **Photo books:** Embrace digital photo technology by creating custom photo books online for about $30 a piece. Select the size, cover, and layout of your book, upload digital photos, add captions, and place your order. The photos and captions are printed directly onto the pages of your hardcover or paperback book. Many Web sites offer photo book creation, including www.mypublisher.com, www.kodakgallery.com, www.shutterfly.com, www.snapfish.com, and www.lulu.com.

Stowing board games

Board games are great for family bonding, lessons in teamwork and taking turns, and having fun. Many board games are classics and, if properly stored, can be passed down to the next generation. Review your collection of board games and follow these guidelines:

- If they're no longer used, consider sharing them with friends or family or donating them to charity.

- If they're missing a significant number of pieces, either contact the manufacturer to order replacement parts or trash them.

- If you want to keep commonly used board games but the boxes are damaged, use masking tape to repair the box or transfer the entire contents of the game to a new box and label it.

After you decide which games to keep, follow these organizational tips:

- Store groups of like-sized games in sturdy plastic containers in your entertainment center, on bookshelves, or in a nearby closet.

- Collect small items that don't stack well, like decks of cards and dice, in a separate box.

Chapter 5

Decluttering Your Kitchen

Traditionally, the kitchen was simply a utilitarian room used for food preparation. Today, the role of the kitchen has expanded to make it the heart of the home — the space where people congregate, meals are prepared together, guests are entertained, home office functions are performed, and days are planned. This is the hardest working room in your home and therefore should be given special attention when organizing. The projects in this chapter help you clear off your counters, make the most of your kitchen's walls and ceilings, and maximize your storage space.

Before you tackle any projects, however, your first step in organizing your kitchen is to determine its goal. Each do-it-yourself organizer will have a different goal for his or her kitchen, depending on how the space is used. When you're determining the goal of your kitchen, consider its functions by answering these questions:

- ✔ Do you entertain in your kitchen? Do you want to?

- ✔ Do you serve meals in your kitchen, dining room, or both?

- ✔ Do you have a small home office in your kitchen?

- ✔ Do your children do homework in your kitchen?

Your kitchen should only store items necessary for its function.

After you determine the goal of your kitchen, the next step is to identify your kitchen's limitations. If you have a newly built home, your kitchen likely has a casual eating area, a pantry (a large one if you're lucky), and possibly even an office nook. You may have all the storage space you need — lucky you! If your kitchen was built in a different era, however, you probably lack storage space and counter space. When you're assessing your space, consider the limitations of your kitchen by answering these questions:

- ✔ Do you have enough cabinet storage for all your dinnerware and appliances?

- ✔ Do you have enough pantry storage for all your food?

- ✔ Is your counter space too limited or crowded for food preparation?

✔ Do you need to store large or rarely used items in a garage or basement?

✔ Do you shop at bulk warehouse stores and require storage for very large items?

Your kitchen can only perform as many functions as the size, layout, and storage space will permit.

After you figure out your kitchen's limitations, it's time to sort. Even a mildly disorganized do-it-yourselfer can benefit from this step! Begin by removing all items from your pantry, cabinets, drawers, closets, and bins. (All that should remain are the items in your refrigerator and freezer.) This crucial step allows you to assess what you have and enables you to quickly eliminate items that don't support your goal or aren't mindful of your kitchen's limitations.

A tried-and-true method is to sort your kitchen items into four large containers labeled as follows:

✔ **STAY:** This item is in good condition, is used often, is relevant to the goal, and will stay in the kitchen. Examples include appliances, pots, pans, plates, and cups.

✔ **MOVE:** This item is in good condition and is used often, but it doesn't support your goal for the kitchen. Examples include sewing kits, photos, sunglasses, and keys.

✔ **SHARE:** This item is in good condition but hasn't been used in the last year, is a duplicate, or no longer serves the kitchen's goal. Examples are mismatched plates, food your family doesn't enjoy, and unused appliances.

✔ **GO:** This item is trash! Examples include expired or stale food and broken items.

Get your whole family involved in sorting the kitchen. Assign your children the task of sorting through their food items, containers, and lunchboxes. Another fun idea is to throw a "happy kitchen party" — invite a few of your close friends over, serve a festive beverage, and get them to help you tackle the kitchen. Don't forget to return the favor and help your friends organize their kitchens!

After you finish sorting, pick out the projects in this chapter that appeal to you, and get started! When you're done, check out the section "The Finishing Touches: Reassembling Your Kitchen" at the end of this chapter for ideas on keeping your kitchen as organized as possible.

Installing an Under-the-Cabinet Paper Towel Holder

Stuff You Need to Know

Toolbox:
- ✔ Pencil
- ✔ Measuring tape
- ✔ Drill
- ✔ Drill bits
- ✔ Screwdriver

Materials:
- ✔ Paper towel holder (with mounting hardware)

Time Needed:
Less than an hour

Home organization is so mainstream nowadays that entire stores are devoted to kitchen organization! You can find specialty appliances and gadgets specifically made to attach to the underside of your cabinets. These products are great because they clear bulky items off your counters!

One quick and easy counter-clearing project is to install a paper towel holder onto the underside of an upper cabinet. The floor of a kitchen cabinet is about ½ inch thick, so you should verify that the length of the screws included with the holder don't exceed the thickness of the holder plus the floor of the cabinet. If they're too long, stop at the hardware store to replace them with shorter screws.

1   Empty the bottom shelf of your cabinet so that you don't drill into anything, especially shelf liners.

Identify the location of your paper towel holder on the underside of your cabinet. Mark the holes onto the underside of your cabinet by sticking a pencil through the screw holes. Use a measuring tape to verify that the hole marks are equidistant from the front edge of the cabinet.

Using a drill bit with a slightly smaller diameter than the screws required for your paper towel holder, drill holes in the marked spots, applying consistent vertical pressure.

Align your paper towel holder's brackets with the holes. Insert the screws into the holes and use a screwdriver to secure the holder in place.

TIP

One benefit of installing an under-the-cabinet paper towel holder is that you'll have more counter space for food prep. Your kitchen will look tidier, too!

Mounting a Message Board

Stuff You Need to Know

Toolbox:

- ✓ Measuring tape
- ✓ Pencil
- ✓ Drill
- ✓ Drill bits
- ✓ Screwdriver
- ✓ Level

Materials:

- ✓ Message board (with mounting hardware)

Time Needed:

Less than an hour

Large home stores, office supply stores, and home improvement centers all sell message boards. An ideal message board has a cork or magnetic area to hang invitations, announcements, and calendars, and a dry-erase/chalkboard area to leave notes for other household members. The board is a great home for frequently used phone numbers, rosters, and activity calendars.

Message boards are available in both vertical and horizontal designs with a wide variety of dimensions. The center of the message board should hang at eye level for adults and approximately 6 to 12 inches below adult eye level for families with younger children. Select a central location for your message board, ideally near the phone in your kitchen. Measure the available space in this location and purchase a message board that fits the space.

1

Determine the vertical center of the frame by measuring the distance from the bottom to the top of the frame, and dividing this measurement by 2. Use a pencil to mark this point in pencil on the backside of the message board.

2

Locate one hanging mechanism on the back of the frame (it's usually a bracket, wire, or tab). With a tape measure, measure the vertical distance between the marked vertical center from Step 1 and the hanging mechanism.

3

Using a pencil, mark the spot on the wall that represents *your* eye-level height. You can determine this height by standing in front of the wall and extending your arm in a straight line from your eye to the wall. If you want a more precise measurement, subtract 3 inches from your height, and then measure that distance up the wall from the floor. In the case of a family with young children, lower this mark by 6 to 12 inches so that they can easily see the board.

What time is soccer practice? What's for dinner tonight? One kid is coming, another is going, and you're left trying to sort out the daily schedule. If you're managing a busy household, I recommend a large message board!

5

Using a drill bit with a slightly smaller diameter than the screw or screws that correspond with the hanging mechanisms, drill a hole into the wall at the spot marked in Step 4, applying consistent horizontal pressure. If your board has more than one hanging mechanism, also drill holes at the other marked spots.

4

Using the measurement obtained in Step 2, measure up from the eye-level height, and mark a second spot at the height at which you will drill the hole for the mounting screw.

Note: If your message board has hanging mechanisms at both upper corners, you have to do a little more measuring! Measure the distance from the vertical center to the top of the message board and the distance from the top center to each corner. After you mark your eye-level height on the wall in Step 3, measure upwards the distance from the vertical center to the top of the board and outwards the distance from the top center to each corner. Use a level to check that your marks are level.

If your message board is extremely heavy, you should drill into a wall stud. See Chapter 3 to find information on locating a wall stud.

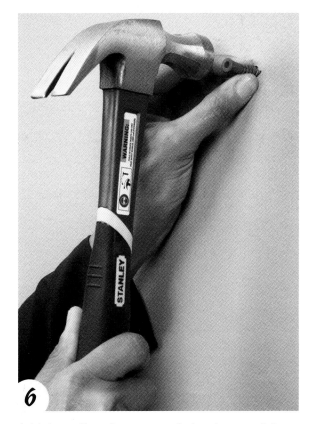

6

Add drywall anchors to any holes that aren't in wall studs. Simply position the drywall anchor into the predrilled hole and tap with a hammer until the anchor is almost completely in the hole.

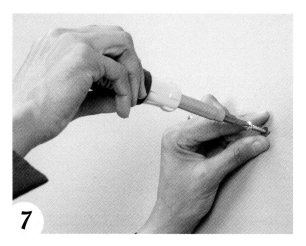

Install your screw or screws into the holes with a screwdriver.

Mount your message board to the wall by connecting the hanging mechanism to the screw. Use your level to ensure that it hangs level.

Organizing your dining room

You can have a family dinner anywhere, from a restaurant to a kitchen island to a local park, but doing it the old-fashioned way — in the dining room — gives you a chance to establish routines and traditions.

People typically use one or two key pieces of furniture to store all their dining needs:

- ✔ **A hutch** is a vertical storage cabinet, generally with glass door cabinets for display and wood door cabinets for storage. A hutch may also have drawers. This furniture piece is ideal if you have a tall or narrow wall space and want to use the height of the wall. It's also beneficial if you want to display your dinnerware or collections.

- ✔ **A buffet** is a horizontal storage cabinet with wood door cabinets and drawers. This piece is a good fit for a dining room with a long wall space. Additionally, because it's table height, your buffet can work as a surface to hold drinks, condiments, and food platters during meals.

Where does everything go?

- ✔ **Glass-front cabinets:** These are for displaying your favorite pieces of china, wine glasses, or family heirlooms! Focus on a few visually interesting pieces rather than trying to store an entire collection in one cabinet. Less is definitely more!

- ✔ **Wood-door cabinets:** Dining room cabinets hold your china, serving platters, and barware. You may find it helpful to maximize this valuable cabinet space by using shelf stackers, china racks, or Lazy Susans (which I discuss later in this chapter). Protect infrequently used china by using padded china storage containers to keep away dust and prevent chipping.

- ✔ **Drawers:** These are for storing all your dining accessories, such as linens, napkin rings, decorations, and small items. Consider dedicating one drawer to linens: Place tablecloths and napkins towards the back of the drawer and collect napkin rings in a small box toward the front of the drawer. A second drawer can be dedicated to accessories like candles and tabletop decorations.

If your space is getting too crowded, transfer infrequently used items or heirlooms to a garage for long-term storage (see Chapter 11). Donate anything you don't use or don't like (I promise I won't tell Grandma!).

Hanging a Utensil Rack

A utensil rack is an example of a kitchen storage device that's both practical and visually pleasing! This kind of rack, which is generally located along your backsplash (that area of wall between the counter and cabinet), holds a few frequently used utensils. Many home stores sell utensil rack sets that include matching utensils for a more put-together look.

Identify the location of your utensil rack. To determine whether there's enough vertical distance to hang your rack between your counter and cabinets (the difference is typically 18 inches), measure the longest utensil you plan to hang. If the item is less than 15 inches (providing a 3-inch clearance), then you have sufficient room to locate your rack in your chosen location. If you plan to hang longer utensils on your rack (such as barbecue tongs), you need to be able to hang it higher on the wall, which means a location void of wall cabinets to allow enough vertical clearance.

2

Hold the rack up to the wall, and use a pencil to mark the spots where you'll drill your holes by pushing the pencil through the screw holes. You may want to use a measuring tape to measure a consistent height, like 2 inches from the top of the upper cabinet to the top of your rack.

3

Use a level to ensure that your marks are level so that your rack won't hang crookedly.

4

Using a drill bit with a slightly smaller diameter than the screws required for mounting the rack, drill holes into the marked spots, applying consistent horizontal pressure.

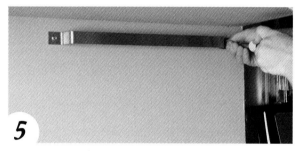

5

Screw your utensil rack into the wall with a screwdriver.

Finding a home for duplicate utensils

After you figure out which of your utensils to hang on your rack, carefully review all the utensils that will go in your utility drawer. As a rule, you should have two or three each of everyday utensils (such as wooden spoons, spatulas, and ladles) and no more than one each of specialty items (such as a meat tenderizer, a garlic press, and a cheese slicer). If you're uncomfortable donating duplicate utensils, consider creating a labeled "Kitchen Box" in your long-term storage area (your garage or attic, most likely). This box can store your surplus can openers, whisks, and the like, and when you're in need of an item or it's time to replace one you've been using regularly, you can start by shopping from your "Kitchen Box."

Hanging Stemware Racks

Stuff You Need to Know

Toolbox:
- ✔ Pencil
- ✔ Drill
- ✔ Drill bits
- ✔ Measuring tape
- ✔ Screwdriver

Materials:
- ✔ Stemware racks (with mounting hardware)

Time Needed:
Less than an hour

Unless you prefer stemless wine glasses, stemware racks are the way to go! Hanging stemware racks are designed to maximize cabinet space and protect your precious stemware. Rails attached to the ceiling of the cabinet have tracks to hold the base of each glass. One rack generally holds two to four glasses, depending on the depth of your cabinet and the base size of your stemware. Standard kitchen cabinets can hold two or three stemware racks — that's up to 12 glasses. Note that some units, like the one featured in this installation, have several tracks attached to a single base.

This project assumes that you're installing the rack inside a cabinet and attaching the rails to the top (ceiling) of the cabinet. See the tip at the end of this project for installing a rack underneath a cabinet.

Place your rack inside your cabinet to plan your installation. Add additional racks, as needed, to store your collection of glasses. Make sure there's enough room to access the stemware on each rack. If your stemware is very bulbous and the mouth is much wider than the base, you need to locate the racks farther apart so the glasses don't touch.

Remember: Each cabinet is different, and you should take into consideration the clearance of the cabinet door, shelf supports, or other specific features of your cabinet. While holding your rack in place, make sure you can easily add and remove your stemware.

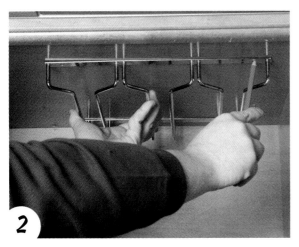

2

Hold the rack up to the ceiling of your cabinet in the location determined in Step 1 and mark the screw holes with a pencil. If you're using multiple racks, leave at least ½ inch of space between racks to easily slide the stemware in and out.

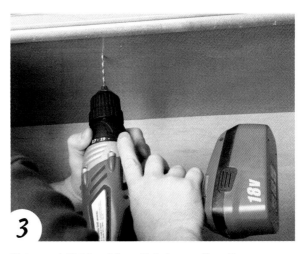

3

Using a drill bit with a slightly smaller diameter than the screws required for your rack, drill holes in the marked spots, applying consistent vertical pressure.

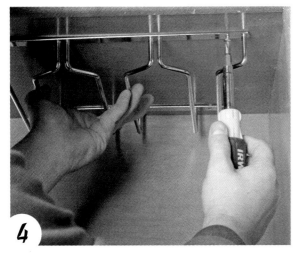

4

Use a screwdriver to screw the rack in place, and then fill the tracks with your stemware.

REMEMBER

You can install stemware racks within a cabinet, with the rails attached to the top (ceiling) of the cabinet, or underneath a kitchen cabinet, with the rails attached to the underside (floor) of the cabinet. Both surfaces are about ½ inch thick. Ensure that the screws provided with your stemware racks aren't so long that they exceed the thickness of the rack plus the ceiling or floor of the cabinet.

TIP

If you choose to install stemware racks on the underside of your kitchen cabinets (above your countertops), note that the frame of the cabinet may be thicker (and therefore extend lower) than the underside of the cabinet. In this case, locate your racks far enough back from the front edge that you can easily slide each glass out of the rack without bumping the base into the frame of the cabinet. I recommend setting the front edge of the rack 4 inches back from the frame.

Installing Pull-Out Bins for Garbage and Recycling

Pull-out bins are a great way to conceal garbage and recycling in a bottom kitchen cabinet or underneath the kitchen sink if there's room. They enable you to hide your trash can when you're entertaining but still access it easily when preparing meals or doing other messy tasks.

Note: Measure the width, depth, and height of your available space before you shop for bins. You need to find bins that fit within the dimension of the cabinet, allowing at least 1-inch clearance on each side.

Determine the placement of your bin frame within your cabinet. To maximize the utility of a wide cabinet, I recommend locating the edge of the frame flush to one side of the cabinet. Use a measuring tape to measure 1 inch from the side of the cabinet wall; mark both the front and the back of the cabinet with a pencil to ensure that your frame will be at an even distance from the side of the cabinet.

2

Align the edge of your frame with the pencil marks made in Step 1. Use your pencil to mark through the holes in the frame to indicate where you'll drill your holes.

3

Using a drill bit with a slightly smaller diameter than the screws required for the frame, drill holes in the marked spots on the floor of the cabinet, applying consistent downward vertical pressure.

4

Align the screw holes in the frame with the drilled holes, and use a screwdriver to screw the frame in place.

5

Connect the rail to the frame by sliding or popping it in place. Place the trash bin into the rail.

Pull-out bins are easy on the back because they enable you to access the entire contents of your cabinet (bins, garbage bags, and so on) with little effort. No more bending and reaching to access the back of the cabinet! Trays also hold the bin firmly in place to make emptying the trash much easier. They're a great solution for the disabled or elderly!

Hanging a Four-Chain, Ceiling-Mounted Pot Rack

Stuff You Need to Know

Toolbox:
- ✔ Ladder
- ✔ Stud finder
- ✔ Pencil
- ✔ Measuring tape
- ✔ Drill
- ✔ Drill bits
- ✔ Pliers or wire cutter

Materials:
- ✔ Pot rack (with mounting and pot-hanging hardware)

Time needed:
Less than half a day

A ceiling-mounted pot rack is both visually interesting and practical! Pots and pans are bulky to store and pose a particular challenge if you have a smaller kitchen with few cabinets. This project frees up tons of cabinet space. The two main styles of support are two-chain (one at either end) and four-chain (one at each corner).

The trick to hanging a stable pot rack is supporting the substantial weight of the loaded up rack from four equal lengths of chain. You attach each chain from the pot rack to a ceiling joist at an outward angle. (Chapter 3 has an introduction to ceiling joists.) To promote stability, your chains should form a rectangle that's wider than the dimensions of the pot rack itself. Angling the chains outward from the center of the pot rack also reduces the amount of swing. This project details the installation of a four-chain, rectangular pot rack.

Before you do anything else, find a buddy to help. This project isn't difficult, but it requires some work on a ladder and heavy lifting.

1 Determine the location of your pot rack, ideally centered over a kitchen island where no one will bump his or her head. If you don't have a kitchen island, locate the pot rack near your cooktop.

Climb your ladder and locate the joists in your chosen location with a stud finder or alternative technique. Mark them in pencil. For this installation, you need to determine which way the joists run (north–south or east–west), and find two to three joists. Ceiling joists are almost always located 16 inches apart.

TIP

A bonus of a ceiling-mounted pot rack is that it can really spruce up your kitchen's décor. Why not embellish your rack with colorful cookware, silk plants, or decorative baskets?

To promote stability, the four hooks installed in the ceiling joists to hold the rack chains will form a rectangle larger than the dimensions of the pot rack itself. The desired location of your pot rack dictates where you install the hanging hooks in the joists.

Measure your pot rack, and transfer that measurement to the ceiling in your desired location. Either center the pot rack between the joists that you marked in Step 2, or align the pot rack with the joists. Starting from the corners of the pot rack dimensions, move 6 inches outward along each joist in either direction and mark these spots. These are the spots where you'll install your hooks into the joists. You should have two pencil marks along one joist and two pencil marks along a second joist. The distance between the joist marks should be wider than the pot rack itself.

If you're struggling with the measurements in this step, you may want to cut out a rectangle the size of the pot rack from newspaper and tape this template to the ceiling. Then make all measurements and marks from the corners of the paper rectangle.

4

Using a drill bit with a slightly smaller diameter than the screws required for the hooks, drill holes into the joists, applying consistent vertical pressure.

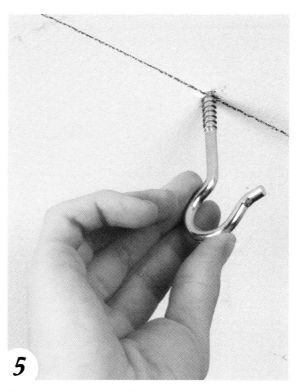

5

Twist the sturdy metal hooks by hand into the ceiling joists.

6

Connect chains to each corner hook on the pot rack. Have someone help you connect each chain to the joists' hooks.

7

Adjust the hanging height of the rack. It should be low enough for you to be able to get pots and pans down but high enough to allow adults to walk underneath it if it isn't hanging over a kitchen island. Check the height, and readjust which links are on the hooks as needed. Then remove the extra links one at a time by using a wire cutter or pliers.

Adding a Wall Rack for Cleaning Tools

Stuff You Need to Know

Toolbox:
- ✔ Measuring tape
- ✔ Pencil
- ✔ Stud finder
- ✔ Level
- ✔ Drill
- ✔ Drill bits
- ✔ Screwdriver

Materials:
- ✔ Cleaning tool rack (with mounting hardware)

Time Needed:
Less than an hour

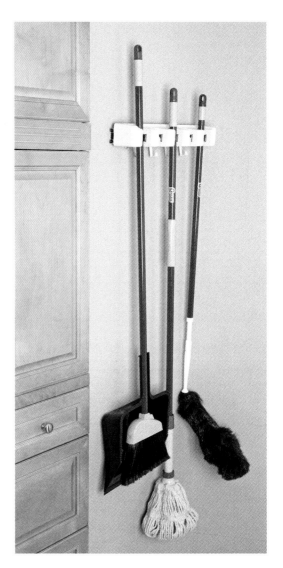

Let's face it — kitchens are messy! With all the food being prepared, served, and consumed, drips, crumbs, and spills inevitably find their way onto the floor. That's why it's convenient to have cleaning tools nearby in a hall closet or pantry to tidy up.

Closets and pantries are tight spaces. Before you shop around for an appropriate rack, select the cleaning implements you plan to hang from it (brooms, dust pans, mops, dusters), and measure the available vertical and horizontal space. Verify that your location has enough height to house your tools and that the width of the rack won't interfere with a door or light switch.

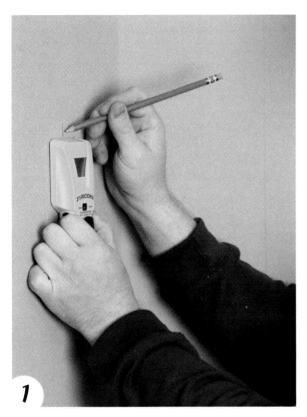

If the rack will hold a significant amount of weight, you should install it into one or more wall studs. Use a stud finder to locate wall studs and mark their location with a pencil.

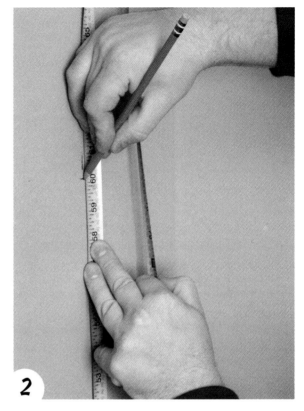

Select the height of the wall rack. I recommend hanging it about 60 inches from the floor to accommodate the length of all your components, and it should be at a convenient height for adults to access. Measure 60 inches along the studs you located in Step 1, and mark the height in pencil.

Hold the rack up to the wall so that one or more hanging mechanisms line up with the wall studs at your desired height marked in Step 2. Push a pencil through the screw holes to mark where you'll drill your holes.

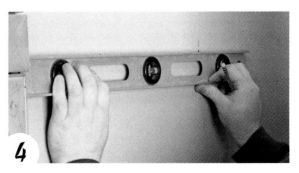

Use a level on the hole marks to ensure that your rack will hang evenly.

5

Using a drill bit with a slightly smaller diameter than the screws required for your rack, drill holes in the marked spots, applying consistent horizontal pressure.

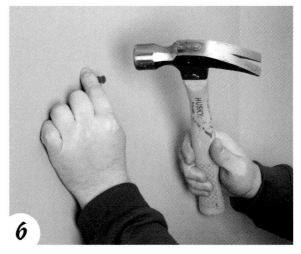

6

Add drywall anchors to any holes that aren't in wall studs. Simply position the drywall anchor in the predrilled hole, and tap it with a hammer until the anchor is almost completely in the hole.

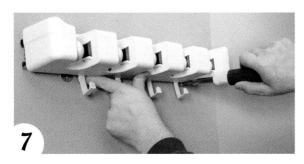

7

Use a screwdriver to screw the rack into the wall.

A wall rack for cleaning tools is also a great place to hang frequently used utility items like flashlights.

Tossing out those plastic storage containers

One of the most common kitchen organization problems is trying to squeeze in too many plastic storage containers! Throw out any container that doesn't have a functional lid, is cracked, or is too bulky to store. I recommend keeping three small round containers, three small rectangular containers, and two large containers. These items are for leftovers and don't deserve to take up more than one shelf of valuable storage space!

Creating a Pantry

If you're struggling to fit all your kitchen items into your kitchen cabinets, consider converting empty wall space into a pantry by adding shelving. Which type of shelving should you choose? Wire shelving (usually plastic-coated) is a budget-friendly choice and provides the greatest visibility of items. Wood shelving is a little tougher on the pocketbook, but it's the strongest option and gives your pantry a professional, clean look.

Note: The two ways to install a shelving system are with or without a horizontal support rail. The main benefit of a horizontal support rail is that you install it and then hook vertical rails into it without further measurement or installation. As long as vertical rails are installed level and at a consistent height, horizontal support rails aren't necessary, though. The drawbacks of using the horizontal rails are that they add to the cost of the project, they can't be used with a sloped ceiling or sloped shelving configuration, and they can give the project an industrial look. This particular project involves shelving installation without horizontal support rails.

Measure the width, height, and depth of the wall space, and then purchase metal rails up to 10 inches less than your vertical wall space. Shelves typically are 4 feet wide, and you need two rails to hold them. If you're installing extra-wide shelving (6 feet wide or more) or have extremely heavy storage requirements, install three vertical metal rails to support the weight. Four-foot shelves are relatively inexpensive, so I recommend using four to six shelves to maximize your storage.

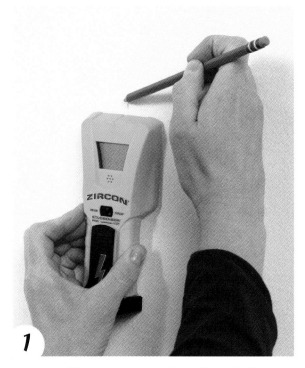

1

Use a stud finder to locate the wall studs. Use your pencil and a level to mark at least two points along one stud, for example, one at eye level and one at knee level. These pencil marks will act as visual cues when installing the metal rail into the wall stud, so spacing them a few feet apart is helpful.

Move 16 inches left or right to locate a second stud and make additional marks. Repeat again if you need a third stud.

The benefit of shelving systems is that you can completely customize them! For example, if you want a 6-inch high shelf to store several dozen baby food jars, this system can accommodate your needs.

2

Position the metal rails according to the preferred height of your wall shelving (remembering that you can adjust the height of each shelf based on where it latches into the rails). The rails should be at least 5 inches above your baseboards and at least 5 inches below the ceiling to allow for maximum shelf storage. (This is where your ladder will come in handy!) Use your pencil to mark the location of the top of each metal rail along the wall stud.

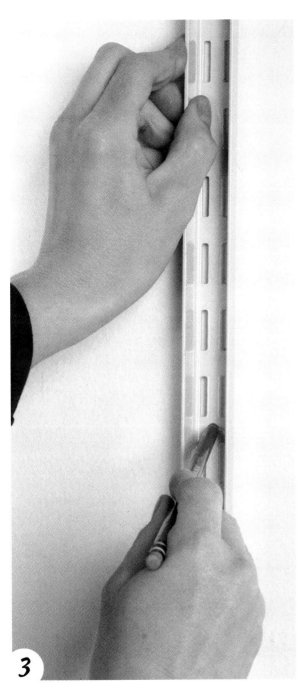

3

Still holding the rail along the first wall stud at the height determined in Step 2, push a pencil through three or four of the screw holes in the rail to indicate where you'll drill into the stud. To help you position additional rails, measure the distance from the top of the baseboard to the screw hole marks (for example, 12 inches, 36 inches, 60 inches, and 72 inches) and note these measurements.

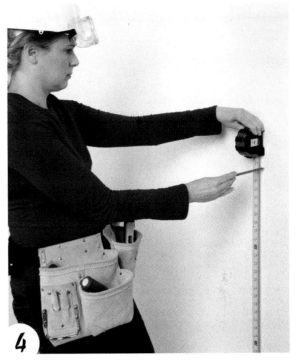

4

On the second wall stud that you located in Step 1, start at the baseboard and measure up the wall stud, marking spots to drill holes at identical heights to your marks for the first rail from Step 3 (for example, 12 inches, 36 inches, 60 inches, and 72 inches). If your shelving will need to support extremely heavy weight, repeat this process for a third rail on a third wall stud.

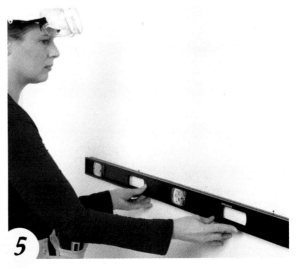

5

Use a level to determine that the screw hole marks for your metal rails are at the same height.

6

Using a drill bit with a slightly smaller diameter than the screws required to install the rails, drill holes in the marked spots, applying consistent horizontal pressure.

7

Align the metal rails with the drilled holes so that the top of the rail is at the height determined in Step 2, and insert the screws. Screw each one in using a screwdriver.

8

Insert the shelving brackets into the notches in the metal rails, making sure to insert the brackets for each shelf into identical height notches on each rail. You can simply set wood or wire shelves onto the brackets or pop them into place.

TIP

Wire baskets are great for organizing collections of small items like spices, seasoning packets, and tea bags. Wire baskets generally hook directly into the rails.

The Finishing Touches: Reassembling Your Kitchen

After you outfit your kitchen to your liking, it's time for the fun and easy part — putting your kitchen back together! In this section, I explain where to stash all your items for maximum ease of use, describe a few handy gadgets for organizing your cabinets, and give you tips on grouping items in your pantry.

Keeping things close at hand

Do you wear a pedometer while preparing meals? Maybe you should! When preparing a meal, you constantly walk between the sink, the stove, and the refrigerator. These three points form the *kitchen triangle.* Minimize extra steps by locating frequently used items in the triangle. Here are some recommendations on placement:

- ✔ Store daily-use plates, bowls, and cups in the upper cabinet closest to the dishwasher to make loading and unloading a breeze. Likewise, silverware goes in the drawer immediately under this cabinet.

- ✔ Children's items go in the lowest possible drawer so they can access them.

- ✔ Dish towels and oven mitts should be in a drawer nearest to the cooktop and oven.

- ✔ Plastic food storage containers, foil, and plastic wrap should be located near the refrigerator to facilitate quickly putting leftovers away.

- ✔ Spices, oils, and vinegars should go in the cabinet nearest the stove. If this location isn't available, you can group these items in your pantry.

Surveying shelf stackers, china and lid racks, and Lazy Susans

When you return items to your cabinets, double-check that they truly support your goal of a tidy, functional space. I recommend locating frequently used items, such as plates and coffee mugs, on the lowest shelves of your upper cabinets. Move infrequently used items, such as small appliances and specialty or seasonal items, to the higher shelves or lower cabinets. If your kitchen cabinets get crowded as you restock them, the following solutions are inexpensive and require no installation:

- ✔ **Shelf stackers** allow short items like coffee mugs and juice glasses to be stacked on two different levels within one shelf. Shelf stackers are generally constructed of a lightweight material like wire or plastic and resemble a small shelf on legs. Short items fit under the shelf stacker as well as on top of the shelf.

- ✔ **China racks** serve a dual purpose of maximizing your cabinet storage and protecting fragile dishes. A china rack is a sturdy wooden base with two rows of pegs. You stand individual dishes between each set of pegs. If you choose to stack your dishes rather than use a china rack, limit your stack to 8 to 12 dishes as not to damage the ones on the bottom of the stack, and consider using a padded china storage set to protect your dishes from dust and chipping.

A family can easily function with only two sets of dishes: everyday and formal. Some families with enough storage may choose to store three sets of dishes: everyday, formal, and holiday. Sets of dishes that are used less than every other year should be donated or passed on to family members who could use a new set of dishes. If you have fragile family heirloom dishes, safely display them or relocate them to long-term storage.

✔ **Lid racks or lid organizers** are invaluable for a crowded drawer of pots and pans. A lid rack is a device similar to a china rack in that it allows you to stack your pot and pan lids vertically and requires no installation. It's constructed of a sturdy wood or wire base with pegs or dividers to separate each lid. Generally, a lid rack is placed at the front of a deep drawer for pots and pans or in an adjacent cabinet. You also can store cookie sheets, platters, and shallow pans in large lid racks.

✔ **A Lazy Susan** is a rotating base on which you place a group of like items in a tight space. The rotating feature allows you to access items from the back of the cabinet quickly by spinning them to the front. An ideal location for a Lazy Susan is in a pantry, where you can store a grouping of sauces, canned foods, or condiments in limited space. Double-decker Lazy Susans are ideal for storing a large collection of spices or vitamins. When serving a meal, use a decorative Lazy Susan to hold salt, pepper, salad dressings, and sauces.

Grouping items in your pantry

An organized pantry can significantly reduce your meal preparation time because you're able to find what you need quickly and easily. If your pantry has at least four shelves, the following is a suggested grouping by shelf:

✔ **Shelf 1 (highest):** NON-FOOD ITEMS (vitamins, cookbooks, recipe cards); SUPPLIES (paper towels, rags, cleaning supplies)

To protect young children and pets, keep potentially hazardous items like vitamins, cleaning supplies, and items in childproof containers on the highest shelf.

✔ **Shelf 2 (close to eye level):** BAKING (flour, sugar, salt, cake mixes, icing, decorations); SAUCES (sauces, unopened salad dressings, condiments)

✔ **Shelf 3 (below eye-level):** DRY FOODS (cereal, rice, pasta, bread, pancake mix); COFFEE/TEA (coffee beans, tea bags, sugar, sweetener, honey)

✔ **Shelf 4 (lowest):** CANNED FOODS (vegetables, fruits); TREATS & SNACKS (cookies, candies, chips, crackers)

Every household functions differently. Ensure that you're taking your preferences (perhaps a daily vitamin taker) and situations (such as young children in the home) into consideration before determining your shelving arrangement.

Add inconspicuous clear labels to the shelves to help you and your family stay on track. You'll find that if a shelf is labeled "CANNED FOODS," you're less likely to squeeze a box of pasta into this space. It's also a good exercise for children, who learn to put items in the labeled space.

Chapter 6

Blissful Bedrooms and Cleansed Closets

Your bedroom is the first thing you see in the morning and the last thing you see before you fall asleep. It's your personal sanctuary, separated from the chaos of your household. Or is it?

Give your bedroom the priority attention it deserves! Having an organized bedroom and a streamlined closet saves you valuable time getting dressed in the morning and will energize you to take on the day. Thoughtful storage options for your clothing make it easier to maintain your system going forward, too.

The bedroom is a major workhorse of your home, so make it work for you. Begin by setting a realistic goal of how you want your bedroom to function. Ideally, your bedroom should be a blissful space free of clutter, work, and projects that allows you to relax. Bedrooms, however, often have limitations such as small size, multiple functions, or improper storage. This chapter helps you make the most of the space and storage you do have and provides clever solutions for additional storage. If your space serves a dual function, such as that of bedroom/home office or bedroom/workout room, I recommend you move the secondary activity elsewhere. There must be somewhere else to store your laptop (see Chapter 8 for home office ideas)!

The goal of a bedroom closet is a visually pleasing and organized space that stores all your clothing, shoes, and accessories. If your closet is properly organized, getting dressed should be simple — and fun! Bedroom closets come in a wide spectrum of sizes — but don't worry, you can transform even the smallest closet into a hardworking space that meets your goal! When you're assessing your space, consider the limitations of your closet by answering these questions:

- ✔ Is your closet large enough for all your clothing? If not, do you have too many clothes?

- ✔ Does your closet lack shelving?

- ✔ Does your closet have enough hanging space for long and short items?

- ✔ Do you have enough storage for your shoes? If not, do you have too many shoes?

- ✔ Do you have sufficient bins, shelves, and hooks for your accessories?

There's nothing like a fresh start when organizing a space! Begin by removing everything from your bedroom and closet. Yes, everything! This crucial step allows you to assess what you have and quickly eliminate items that don't support your goal or aren't mindful of the limitations of your room and closet. It's time to sort your items! Divide your items into four large containers labeled as follows:

- **STAY:** This item is in good condition, is used often, is relevant to the goal, and will stay in the bedroom or closet. For the bedroom, this means furniture that's appropriately sized for your space, fits your needs, and is in good condition. (Obviously you won't be able to fit furniture in the STAY container, but you get the idea.) For the closet, this means clothes that you love and wear often.

- **MOVE:** This item doesn't belong in your bedroom (such as exercise equipment and work projects), or it needs to be removed from the bedroom until it has been fixed (think broken furniture). Likewise, items in the closet (such as memorabilia, electronics, and photos) need to be returned to their proper rooms or removed until they're repaired (such as stained, torn, or ill-fitting clothing).

- **SHARE:** This item is in good condition but no longer serves the goal, so you should share it! For the bedroom, this includes extra pieces of furniture or accessories that are just cluttering up the space. For the closet, you should donate items that you haven't worn in 12 months. Examples of items to share are those that you don't wear anymore (like last year's jeans or business clothing that's too formal for your work environment), items that don't fit (like skinny jeans or maternity clothes), and items that are outdated (like your college jeans).

- **GO:** This item is trash — don't even try to donate this junk! Examples include items that are permanently stained, worn out, or beyond repair. If you wouldn't pass it on to a loved one or friend, you shouldn't donate it!

Creating a soothing atmosphere in your bedroom

These décor do's and don'ts help keep your eyes on the prize: a bedroom that you want to spend time in!

- Do incorporate a wide variety of textures in your room. For example, a shaggy throw rug, velvety drapes, and fringed throw pillows add layers of interest and warmth to your space.

- Do set up a radio, CD player, or MP3 player to help you achieve bliss through soothing classical or instrumental background music at the touch of a button.

- Do make your bed each day. At the end of a long day, you'll return to your bedroom with a smile!

- Do add scent to your bedroom. Scented candles or essential oil diffusers can instantly transform your mood through aromatherapy. For example, lavender is relaxing, peppermint is energizing, and sage is sensual.

- Don't leave any clothing, shoes, or laundry on the floor. Clothing clutter is distracting and doesn't enhance your bedroom bliss. If you don't have time to put away your clothing before you rush out the door, at least get it into the closet.

Building a Homemade Nightstand

Every bedroom has a bed, but does every bedroom have a nightstand? An essential yet often overlooked piece of furniture, a nightstand is a surface to stow a book or a pair of reading glasses, set a glass of water, or situate a reading lamp and an alarm clock. This project is a fun and inexpensive way to create a nightstand out of common household items. I recommend using a sturdy trash can (either round or square) as the base and a piece of wood (with a larger diameter than the base) as the top. Then pick a fabric to disguise the base; I recommend selecting a neutral fabric that doesn't compete with your bedding, and use one that's lightweight, like cotton, but substantial enough to disguise the base!

1 Prepare a well-ventilated painting area (like a garage with the door open) by laying down dropcloths or newspaper to protect the workspace.

2 Use a stir stick to completely mix the paint or stain you plan to use on the round piece of wood that will be your nightstand top. Use a paintbrush or sponge brush to apply the paint or stain to the wood. Wipe off the excess paint or stain as needed, and let the wood dry completely. (You may need to apply one to two coats to achieve your desired look.)

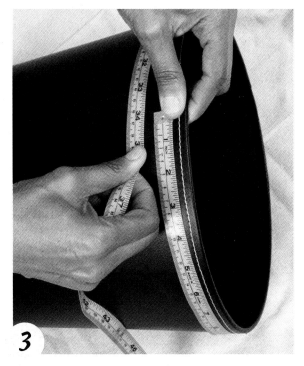

3

Use a flexible measuring tape to measure the perimeter of your base (the distance around the outside edge). Add 4 inches to this measurement to determine the length of your fabric.

4

Measure the height of the base of your table, from the floor to the top edge. Add 2 inches to this measurement to determine the width of your fabric.

5

Use a flexible measuring tape and a piece of chalk to mark your fabric with the measurements from Steps 3 and 4. You'll wrap the nightstand base in a single rectangular piece of fabric.

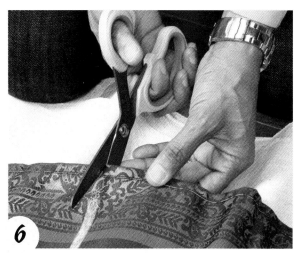

6

Use fabric scissors to cut the fabric to size along your chalk line from Step 5. (Fabric scissors give you a crisp, clean cut through fabric.)

7

Create a ½-inch fold at the top edge of the length side of the fabric (the side that corresponds to the perimeter plus 4 inches). Iron this fold to create a crisp edge. Repeat on the opposite side of the fabric, ironing a ½-inch fold along the bottom edge of the length.

8

Turn your trash can base upside down so the open end is facing down. Starting anywhere along the edge of the top of the base, use a hot glue gun to glue the ironed hem of your fabric to the base to create a fabric skirt around your base. Proceed to glue the ironed hem of the fabric around the entire perimeter of the base, and overlap the remaining 4 inches to create a flap to allow you to access any hidden lower storage (see the tip at the end of this project). The fabric should be glued to the base only along the top edge of the base.

9

If you want the wood top permanently attached to the base, add a few small beads of hot glue to the perimeter edge of the top of the base, and then quickly position the wood on the base. (You also can use double-sided adhesive foam squares for a light hold.)

Interested in other options for your nightstand base and top? If you're looking for concealed lower storage, I suggest using a collection of plastic crates turned on their sides as your base; if you want a pedestal-style table, choose an attractive garden planter, large vase, or urn. If the base is attractive, you don't need a fabric cover for the base. Options for your top include a decorative piece of wood, a wrought-iron trivet, a round piece of glass, or a colorful ceramic platter. You have to get creative when attaching the base to the top; depending on the top you select, you can use hot glue, gorilla glue, screws, or putty.

Coloring your closet

If you ever find yourself with a completely empty closet, make the most of this unique situation and transform your closet space with paint.

✔ For a calm feeling, try light blues or greens.

✔ To feel energized, try a spicy orange, magenta, or turquoise.

✔ For a traditional feel, stick to neutral beige or gray tones.

✔ Consider adding wallpaper to a single wall to create a boutique look!

Mounting a Wall Rack

Stuff You Need to Know

Toolbox:
- Measuring tape
- Pencil
- Level
- Drill
- Drill bits
- Screwdriver

Materials:
- Rack (with mounting hardware)

Time Needed:
Less than an hour

Wall-mounted closet racks are a simple way to organize your accessories, clothing, and hats. Closet racks tend to be more decorative — like wrought-iron or painted wood — rather than utilitarian because they usually only hold a collection of lighter items like scarves or belts. Use one or more racks to maximize accessory storage along the wall of your closet or in the often overlooked wall space behind your closet door.

1 Determine the location of your rack. Ideally, you should hang it at eye level or above so that it can hold longer, floor-length items. Measure the height on the wall with a measuring tape and mark it with a pencil.

2

Hold the rack to the wall at your selected height, and push a pencil through the screw holes of the hanging mechanism to show you where to drill holes.

3

Use a level on the hole marks to ensure that the rack will hang level.

4

Using a drill bit with a slightly smaller diameter than the screws required to hang the rack, drill holes in the marked spots, using consistent horizontal pressure.

5

Screw your rack into the wall with a screwdriver.

If you only need to hang a single heavy item like a terry robe or bulky coat, use a wall hook mounted in a wall stud instead of a wall rack. (Chapter 7 has instructions on mounting a hook.)

Creating a Door-Mounted Accessories Organizer

Why stop at clothes? With proper planning, your bedroom closet can store your clothes, shoes, scarves, belts, hats, and jewelry! The back of the closet door is often unclaimed real estate and an ideal spot to locate an accessories organizer.

Before you run out and buy your components, identify the items you want to store on your organizer; good candidates are hats, scarves, belts, ties, bangle bracelets, bandanas, and even boas! Sort your accessories into groups to determine the number and type of hanging mechanisms you need. Purchase racks and hooks that are the right size for each group of accessories. Decorative racks less than 24 inches wide are best for holding a collection of items like scarves or belts; you drill holes and screw them directly into the door. Door hooks can be hung over the door (no installation), twisted in, or stuck on with adhesive, and they're best for short or lightweight individual items like baseball caps or bracelets. Because accessories tend to be lightweight, you can purchase plastic hooks (reserve the heavy-duty hooks for garage or entryway use). Hangers designed to hold belts or ties can be mounted to the back of the door and are an excellent solution for holding long items.

1

Determine the vertical layout of your organizer based on the items each element will hold: Items that are short and a consistent length (like bangle bracelets or hats) should be located highest on the door. Items that are long and vary in size (like scarves or belts) should be located lowest on the door. Just be sure that your lowest items won't drag on the floor every time you open and close the door.

2

To create a visually pleasing organizer, use a measuring tape to center each hanging mechanism on the door. If you're attaching an even number of components, such as two adhesive hooks, use your measuring tape to hang these the same distance from the center of the door to create a uniform look. Mark each location in pencil.

3

Starting with the highest group, hold up your rack and use a pencil to mark through the screw holes. Repeat this step for components that you'll place on lower parts of the door.

4

If you're screwing a rack into the door, fit your drill with a drill bit with a slightly smaller diameter than the screws required to mount the rack. Also, the drill bit shouldn't be longer than the door is thick, or you'll end up with holes straight through your door.

Drill holes in the marked spots for screwed-in racks, applying consistent horizontal pressure.

5

Screw all racks into the door using a screwdriver.

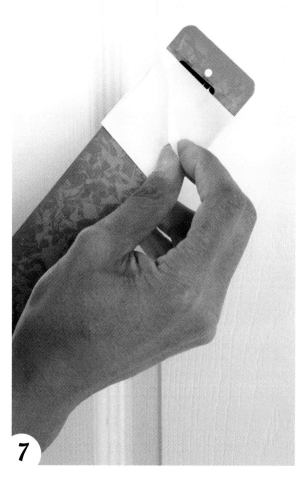

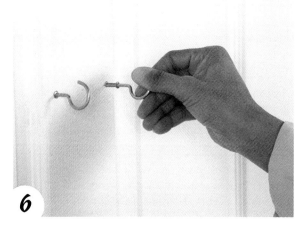

6

Attach hooks by hanging them over the door, sticking them to the door with adhesive squares, or twisting them directly into holes drilled into the door using the technique described in Step 4.

7

Mount any specialty hangers using adhesive squares or hooks.

You've put on your slacks, your blouse, your jacket, and your shoes. But are you *dressed?* Adding accessories like belts and scarves is the fun part! Accessories often are stashed in boxes in the far recesses of closets, making them difficult to access daily. A big perk of an organizer is that you can view your entire collection of accessories at once and easily select the right piece for your outfit.

Installing Shoe Shelving

Shoes are no longer just mere footwear. If you are a woman, are married to a woman, or have ever met a woman, there's a very good chance you understand what I'm talking about. Shoes are expensive! They deserve to be off the floor of your closet and on a pedestal . . . or at least on a wall-mounted shoe rack! This is a simple project that will make you — or the woman in your life — very, very happy. You create a wall-mounted shelving system from two vertical metal rails, brackets that snap in place, and several rows of wood shelving. (Similar shelving systems for heavier items, like those in garages or pantries, may require more than two vertical support rails.)

Before you shop for supplies and begin installation, measure the wall space you have in your closet and determine the number of shelves you need or can accommodate. You need at least 24 inches of available width; a 24-inch shelf holds three to four pairs of shoes, and a 36-inch shelf holds five to six pairs. As for height, your metal rails should be at least 5 inches above your baseboards and at least 5 inches lower than the ceiling to accommodate shoes while maximizing shelf storage. Plan different shelf heights for flats (position shelves about 6 inches apart) and heels (position shelves about 10 inches apart), and for tall footwear like boots, you may want to keep them on the floor and place the lowest shelf at a height of 18 inches or more.

1

Locate a wall stud in your chosen location with a stud finder. Use your level and a pencil to mark the stud at a minimum of two heights — maybe knee height and eye level. These marks will help you position the vertical metal rail along the wall stud.

2

Measure and move 16 inches to either side to locate a second stud (they're usually 16 inches apart). Repeat Step 1 on this stud.

3

Position the first metal rail vertically along one wall stud at the desired height. Position your level alongside the rail to verify that it's exactly vertical.

TIP

If your shoes are in various locations throughout your closet — or worse, multiple closets throughout your house — remembering exactly what you own can be challenging. You're likely to forget you own a certain pair (like red flats) and may end up buying a replacement pair you don't need! Shoe shelving in your closet lets you consolidate your collection and select the right pair for any outfit.

4

Use your pencil to mark through the screw holes in the rail to indicate where you'll drill your holes. These marks don't correspond to the height of the shelves; they're merely to screw the rail to the wall stud. Repeat with the second metal rail, marking through the same screw holes as on the first rail.

5

Use a level to verify that the screw hole marks from Step 4 are at consistent heights. This is very important because level vertical rails ensure that you have level shelves!

6

Using a drill bit with a slightly smaller diameter than the screws required for the vertical rails, drill holes in all the marked spots, applying consistent horizontal pressure.

7

Align the holes in the metal rail with the drilled holes, and screw the rail in with a screwdriver. Repeat for the second rail.

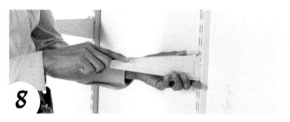

8

Insert the shelving brackets into the notches in the metal rails, making sure that you use the same notches in both rails.

9

Set wood shelves onto the brackets or pop them into place. (If your shelving system has wire shelves, this step should be the same.)

Adding High and Low Closet Rods

It's time to make some decisions for your closet organization . . . namely, one rod or two? For maximum storage, consider using a double rod, which consists of a short low rod and a full-length high rod. This configuration allows full-length garments to hang from the part of the high rod that extends beyond the shorter low rod. The low rod needs to be high enough that shirts and skirts don't skim the floor; I recommend 38 to 40 inches from the floor. The high rod should be hung at twice the height of the low rod to allow shirts and skirts enough clearance from the low rod; I recommend 76 to 80 inches from the floor. You're free to experiment with different heights that work for your closet.

In this project, the high rod is the same length as the back wall of the closet and is installed directly into the side walls using sockets. This type of rod can be expandable or cut to fit the length of the back wall. If the rod is longer than 4 feet, you need brackets in the middle of the rod to distribute the weight. I recommend adding a support bracket every 16 or 32 inches in order to hit wall studs.

In this project, the low rod spans about half the length of the back wall of the closet and connects to the wall with a socket on one end. The low rod needs to be suspended by brackets that support the middle of the bar and the end that isn't installed into a side wall socket. I recommend adding a support bracket every 16 or 32 inches in order to hit wall studs.

1

Identify the desired height of your clothing rods. You should select a height between 38 inches (minimum for a low rod) and 80 (maximum for a high rod), making sure that you can reach to get clothes on and off the high rod in particular. Use a pencil to mark the wall in several locations at your desired heights.

Make the most of your closet space by grouping like items together, using uniform hangers and leaving space between each item (see the later section "The Finishing Touches: Reassembling Your Bedroom and Closet" for details). If your clothing is still packed together too tightly, consider adding another clothing rod.

2

Locate a wall stud on the back wall of your closet with a stud finder, and mark it with a pencil. (Chapter 3 tells you how to find a wall stud.)

3

Move 16 inches to either side to locate and mark an additional stud. Repeat along the span of the closet wall.

4

Determine the locations of your brackets on the wall studs at both high (rod) and low (rod) levels. Hold each bracket against the wall and use a pencil to mark the screw holes so that you know where to drill holes for mounting the bracket.

Note: Clothing rods are weighed down with clothing, and additional brackets are necessary to support the weight of closet rods longer than 4 feet. Remember that wall studs are located at 16-inch intervals, so your brackets should be located every 16 or 32 inches.

6

Using a drill bit with a slightly smaller diameter than the screws required for your brackets, drill holes in all the marked spots, applying consistent horizontal pressure.

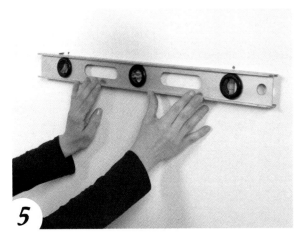

5

Use your level to verify that all pencil marks are level for both the high rod and the low rod.

7

Align the screw holes in the brackets with the holes in the wall, and use a screwdriver to screw your brackets into the wall.

8

Temporarily place the high clothing rod on its brackets so you can see exactly where the sockets should be positioned on the adjacent walls. Trace around the rod where it meets the side walls.

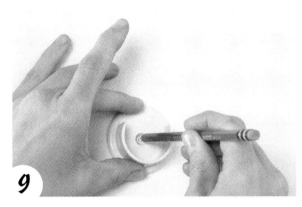

9

Remove the high clothing rod so you can install your sockets. Hold each socket in place (where you traced the rod in Step 8), and mark the screw holes in the sockets so you know where to drill holes.

10

Using a drill bit that's slightly smaller than the screws required for the sockets, drill holes in the marked spots, applying consistent horizontal pressure.

11

Align the screw holes in the sockets with the holes in the wall, and use a screwdriver to screw your sockets in the wall, positioning them with the opening facing upward. This open-ended design allows you to easily lower the rod into the socket.

12

Install your high clothing rod by lowering it into the sockets.

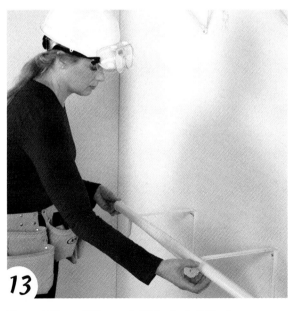

13

Repeat Steps 8 through 12 to install the lower clothing rod. Note that the lower clothing rod only spans a portion of the wall and is supported by a wall socket at one end and a bracket at the other.

The Finishing Touches: Reassembling Your Bedroom and Closet

Pat yourself on the back because the hard work is done: Your wardrobe is streamlined, and your bedroom and closet boast plenty of new storage options. All that's left are the finishing touches. This section presents some easy and rewarding solutions to give your space a polished look.

Storing items under the bed

If you're sleeping on a king-size bed that measures 76 inches by 80 inches and is approximately 9 inches off the floor, you have more than 31 square feet of unused storage underneath your bed! The space underneath the bed is often underutilized, so check out some ways to make the most of your newfound space:

- **Bed risers:** Bed risers can elevate your bed an additional 6 inches — creating an additional 21 square feet of storage space! Purchase an extra long bedskirt to hide unsightly storage down below.

- **Storage containers:** For customized storage, you can build wood boxes on wheels (detailed in Chapter 9). Otherwise, you can purchase under-the-bed containers in varying sizes and made of a variety of materials like plastic or canvas. Prevent damage from moths and mildewing by storing infrequently used or delicate items in plastic zippered bags.

  - For a carpeted bedroom, I recommend purchasing several plastic under-the-bed boxes.

  - For hardwood or laminate floors, I recommend purchasing fabric or canvas storage containers that won't scratch your flooring.

- **Arrangement of storage containers:** Play around with the arrangement of multiple storage boxes under the bed to maximize the space. Store frequently used items (such as extra sheet sets) under the perimeter of the bed and seasonal items (such as bulky winter sweaters or blankets) toward the middle of the space. Hide holiday or birthday presents for young kids in the center area where they'll be hidden by the perimeter storage and harder for curious little ones to access.

Dresser drawer do's and don'ts

When properly organized, dresser drawers can store a ton of clothing and accessories! One perk of using drawers is that items like t-shirts or tank tops never fall off hangers and end up in a wrinkled pile on the floor of your closet. Another perk is that you can neatly tuck an entire collection of items, like exercise wear, into a single drawer. Follow this list of do's and don'ts to make the most of the drawer space you do have:

✔ **Do store all non-hanging items in your drawers.** These items include undergarments, nylons, slips, socks, pajamas, exercise wear, bathing suits, and casual t-shirts.

✔ **Do dedicate each drawer to a type of clothing.** If you have several small drawers at the top of your dresser, you can assign them socks, undergarments, nylons and slips, and swimwear. If you only have large drawers, you can use vertical drawer dividers to separate one drawer into several sections. Drawer dividers are wood or plastic vertical slats that expand to fit your drawers; you can purchase them at large home stores and organization stores.

✔ **Do use drawer nooks to organize smaller items like socks or undergarments.** Drawer nooks use a grid to divide an individual drawer into 12 to 20 squares. You can purchase drawer nooks at large home stores and organization stores.

✔ **Do keep clothing in neat stacks to maximize drawer space.** A narrow drawer (perhaps about 15 inches wide) may hold only one stack of folded items, like t-shirts, whereas a standard drawer (about 30 inches) may hold two stacks and an extra wide drawer (more than 40 inches) three stacks of clothing.

✔ **Do add fragrance sachets, cedar chips, or scented drawer liners to keep your drawers and their contents smelling fresh!**

✔ **Don't try to store jeans or slacks in your dresser drawers.** Adult pants are very bulky, and a few pairs will fill an entire drawer! Instead, purchase specialty hangers that efficiently hang up to five pants on a single hanger (see the later section "Arranging your clothes neatly").

✔ **Don't store non-clothing items such as books, memorabilia, and toiletries in your dresser drawers.** Dresser drawer space is valuable and should be reserved for clothing!

✔ **Don't overstuff your drawers!** If a drawer can't easily slide in and out, the top item of clothing will stick and topple over your tidy stacks of clothing.

Hanging ties and belts

If you haven't already committed to hanging your ties and belts on wall hooks or racks, for under $10 you can purchase tie/belt hangers that store your ties and belts vertically in small or large groups (see Figure 6-1).

These clever devices were designed to store ties and belts, but you can also use them for the following items:

✔ Scarves and wraps

✔ Necklaces and bracelets

✔ Nightgowns and slips

Figure 6-1: Tie and belt hangers keep your accessories organized.

Arranging your clothes neatly

Coordinated hangers provide a pleasing order to your closet as well as ensure that there's enough space between items for them to hang properly. You can purchase inexpensive matching plastic hangers at large discount stores or opt for more expensive wooden or fabric-lined hangers.

Instead of throwing them away, return all your wire hangers to your local dry cleaner. They'll appreciate it, and you'll be doing something good for the environment!

Home organization stores and Web sites also offer specialty hangers to capture just about any type of clothing imaginable. Try these options (and check out Figure 6-2):

- If your clothing rod space is at a premium, tiered specialty hangers (with or without clips) are a great solution. They group items together vertically, so one hanger can support five to seven pants or skirts. Think of the valuable inches of hanging space you'll save.

- An open-ended hanger provides one open end for easy removal of dress slacks, shawls, and wraps. This is a great solution for frequent travelers because they can pack several pairs of slacks at a time without removing a single hanger from the closet rod.

Figure 6-2: Specialty hangers help you organize your clothing and save space.

Another trick of the trade is to present clothing in a manner that's both pleasing to the eye and facilitates finding the item you want. Group all your hanging items by type. To be more specific, order them as follows from left to right:

- Coats, casual
- Coats, dressy
- Sweaters, casual
- Sweaters, dressy
- Long-sleeve shirts, casual
- Long-sleeve shirts, dressy
- Short-sleeve shirts, casual
- Short-sleeve shirts, dressy
- Tank tops, casual
- Tank tops, dressy

If you want to further customize your hanging clothes, you can organize each sub-group by color. Organization is addictive, isn't it?

After you've grouped your clothing, why not try clothing dividers to keep everything separate? Clothing dividers are white plastic discs that you place on your closet rods (see Figure 6-3). They're extremely inexpensive and sold at home organization stores. Like labels on storage boxes, they provide a constant reminder of where each item belongs and will help keep your system intact. There's nothing more frustrating than taking the time to set up an organizational system only to have to redo it months later!

Figure 6-3: Distinguish groups of clothing with dividers.

People think they wear all the clothes in their closet when really only about 30 to 50 percent is worn regularly. Don't worry; I can help! Group all your shirts together in your closet, and then after wearing a shirt, return it to the far right of the group. Over time, all your favorite shirts will naturally move to the right, and all those shirts not being worn will remain on the left. You'll be able to pare down your wardrobe by searching from left to right. Employ this process with the other items in your closet for optimal results.

Chapter 7

Up, Off, and Away! Organizing Your Bathroom

Bathrooms aren't large in volume, but they have to store large volumes of stuff! Often your current storage is maxed out and you need clever organizational solutions for storing bathroom necessities. The projects in this chapter focus on eliminating counter clutter, efficiently organizing drawers, and wall-mounting as much as possible!

A typical bathroom has makeup, toiletries, toothbrushes, towels, and clutter covering the counter. Get that stuff *up, off,* and *away!* The goal in this chapter is to make your daily prep time in your bathroom as productive as possible by having all your storage *up* on the walls, all your clutter *off* the counter, and all your counter clutter put *away.* You'll love the results.

The biggest limitation of a bathroom is obvious — its small size. But overcoming this limitation is easy with storage mounted on the walls. Wall-mounted storage increases the square footage of your bathroom by reducing the footprint of armoires or storage towers. The *footprint* is simply the square footage of floor space that an item occupies. For example, a 2-x-3-foot storage armoire in the bathroom takes up about 6 square feet of usable floor space, whereas a wall-mounted cabinet above the toilet doesn't take up any usable floor space! In a small space like a bathroom, every inch counts.

After you know your bathroom's goal and limitations, you need to assess its contents. Begin by emptying all cabinets and drawers and collecting counter clutter. This step allows you to evaluate the contents of your bathroom and toss anything that doesn't belong. Sort your trove of toiletries and treasures into four large containers labeled:

- ✔ **STAY:** This item is in good condition, is used often, is relevant to the goal, and should stay in the bathroom. Examples include toiletries, cosmetics, cleaning supplies, and bathroom linens.

- ✔ **MOVE:** This item is in good condition and is used often, but it doesn't belong in the bathroom. Examples are electronics, clothing, and tools.

✔ **SHARE:** This item is in good condition but hasn't been used in the last year, is a duplicate, or no longer serves the room's goal. Examples include outdated jewelry, unopened beauty products, extra hair styling tools, and gently used linens.

✔ **GO:** Dump it! Examples are expired cosmetics, beauty products you don't like or use, and broken items.

After you sort your bathroom's contents, choose the projects that will help you effectively store what's in the "STAY" container, and get to work! When you're done, check out the section "The Finishing Touches: Reassembling Your Bathroom" at the end of this chapter for ideas on keeping your bathroom tidy.

Lookin' good: Organizing your makeup

Face it: Appearance is important! On average, people spend close to an hour every day selecting clothing, styling hair, and applying makeup. The easiest way to streamline this process is to whittle your makeup supply down to a reasonably sized collection of items that are used regularly and in good condition. In my experience, women have a hard time letting go of makeup, so I offer some advanced sorting guidelines to shave valuable minutes off your morning routine:

✔ Throw away anything that you don't wear or don't like.

✔ Discard any product that has been used down to the nub. Buy a new one if you like it so much!

✔ Any makeup from back in the day has to go (you know what I mean — iridescent blue eye shadow, creamsicle-orange lipstick, and the like).

✔ Follow the tips at beauty.about.com/od/makeuptrickstips/a/shelflife.htm and throw away any makeup that's past its expiration date, as follows:

- Mascara: 4 months

- Foundation and concealer: 1 year

- Nail polish: 1 year

- Eye liner and lip liner: 3 years

- Lipstick: 2 years

- Eye shadow: 3 years

After you've gone through your makeup, purchase a cosmetics organizer for your drawer. These organizers are generally made of acrylic or plastic and have several divided compartments (in different sizes and shapes) to organize your products. Group like items together based on what you use them on or for:

✔ Lips: Lipstick, lip liner, lip gloss

✔ Eyes: Eye shadow, eyeliner, mascara

✔ Face: Lotion, foundation, concealer, blush, powder

✔ Tools: Tweezers, brushes, sharpeners

Mounting a Wall Hook

Stuff You Need to Know

Toolbox:

- ✔ Measuring tape
- ✔ Stud finder
- ✔ Pencil
- ✔ Level
- ✔ Drill
- ✔ Drill bits
- ✔ Screwdriver

Materials:

- ✔ Hook (with mounting hardware)

Time Needed:
Less than an hour

Scented candles and soft classical music. A glass of wine. A soak in a whirlpool bath tub with a trashy romance novel. You emerge from a leisurely bath, reach for your crumpled, moist bathrobe on the floor . . . wait a minute!

If you want a wrinkle-free, dry, cozy robe (and who doesn't?), a wall-mounted hook is the solution! No bathroom is complete without a sturdy hook for bath towels and robes. Thick, absorbent fabrics like terry cloth can add a lot of weight to a hook, so I recommend that you install hooks into wall studs.

Determine where to hang your hook, and use a measuring tape to verify that your chosen spot is high enough that your towels and robe won't brush the floor. I recommend hanging your hook at least 65 inches off the floor to accommodate a full-length robe or nightgown.

Locate a wall stud with a stud finder. Mark the stud with a pencil at the height determined in Step 1.

Do you have a bad back? Using wall-mounted devices like wall hooks can help you keep items at arm's length. (You also can transfer frequently used items from lower cabinets to upper cabinets to prevent excessive bending.)

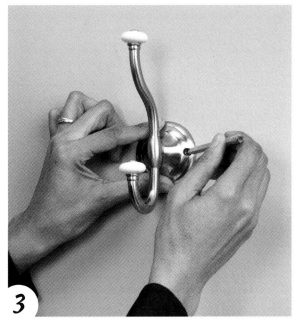

Use a level to make sure the holes you've marked are level. Single hooks usually have two horizontal holes, and double hooks usually have two vertical holes. Turn your level horizontally or vertically as needed to check your marks.

Hold the hook up to the wall stud, and use a pencil to mark the location of the holes you need to drill by sticking the pencil through the screw holes.

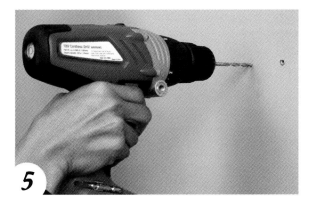

Using a drill bit with a slightly smaller diameter than the screws required for your hook, drill holes in the marked spots, applying consistent horizontal pressure.

Screw your hook into the wall with a screwdriver.

You have a choice of a single hook or a double hook (two prongs attached to one base). The decision is yours!

Installing a Towel Bar

Every bathroom in your home is probably already equipped with at least one towel bar. If this bar is working overtime by holding towels for multiple people, why not install another? Alternatively, you can give your space an inexpensive lift by upgrading all the towel racks.

1 Determine the location and height of your towel bar. If you plan to hang bath towels on the bar, hang it as close to the shower as possible to reduce dripping on your floor. If you plan to hang hand towels on the bar, hang it as close to the sink as possible. The standard height of towel bars in new homes is 48 inches off the floor, but you can tailor this height to fit the needs of your household.

2 Locate the wall studs with a stud finder, and mark them with a pencil.

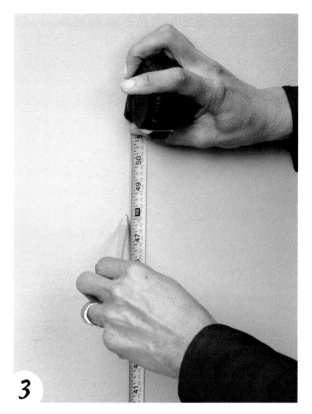

3 Use a measuring tape and pencil to mark the height of the towel bar along the stud.

4 Hold the towel bar up to the wall at the height determined in Step 3 so that one hanging mechanism is over a stud (see the tip at the end of this project), and use a pencil to lightly trace around both hanging mechanisms.

Note: You can't mark the exact screw holes yet because they're concealed by the towel bar. This step is to determine the spacing of the hanging mechanisms.

5 Use your level to check the pencil marks made in Step 4 to ensure that your towel bar will hang level.

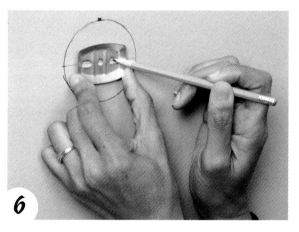

6 Detach the hanging mechanisms from the towel bar with a screwdriver. Hold one hanging mechanism to the wall in the spot marked in Step 4, and mark the screw holes with a pencil. Start with the mechanism that aligns with a stud.

7 Using a drill bit with a slightly smaller diameter than the screws required for the hanging mechanism, drill holes in the marked spots, applying consistent horizontal pressure.

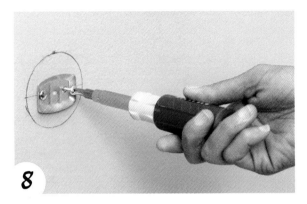

8

Use a screwdriver to screw the first hanging mechanism into the stud.

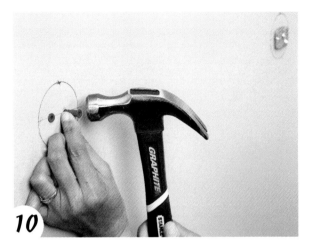

10

If your holes in Step 9 aren't drilled into wall studs, insert drywall anchors to strengthen the installation. Simply position the drywall anchor in the predrilled hole and tap with a hammer until the anchor is almost completely in the hole.

9

Hold the second hanging mechanism to the wall in the spot marked in Step 4, and mark the screw holes with a pencil. Drill holes in the marked spots, applying consistent horizontal pressure.

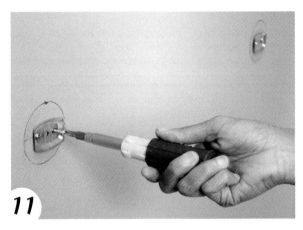

11

Use a screwdriver to screw the second hanging mechanism into the drywall anchors if you used them. Otherwise screw into the predrilled holes in the wall stud.

TIP

A new towel bar doesn't need to be the same exact model as other towel bars in the bathroom, but try sticking with the same type of finish (such as brass, nickel, black, white, or oak).

Use a small screwdriver to firmly screw the towel bar to the hanging mechanisms.

Because of the towel bar width and stud spacing, you may not be able to mount both hanging mechanisms into studs; getting one into a stud and one into drywall will suffice as long as you use drywall anchors. However, if the second hanging mechanism is located exactly 16 inches away from the first one, you can mount both mechanisms into studs and eliminate the need for dry-wall anchors.

Bed, bath, and beyond! Organizing your linen closet

Linen closets are usually located near bath-rooms, laundry rooms, and bedrooms. If you're lucky enough to have one (or more than one, which would be really lucky), this space acts as a home for all your bed and bath linens and frees up your bedroom clos-ets for storing clothing. If roomy enough, a linen closet can also store table linens, beach towels, and sleeping bags. And if yours is located on a different floor than your garage, it may also be a great spot to store a small collection of utility items (the following list has some examples). *Remember:* Protect infrequently used items by placing them in garment bags or zipped plastic storage bags before you store them.

As a general rule, linen closet storage is structured by shelf height and by item size. For this purpose, I assume you're facing a linen closet with five shelves at fixed heights. If you have adjustable shelves, feel free to reconfigure to your exact needs!

- ✔ **Shelf 1 (highest shelf):** This shelf is slightly hard to reach, so it's a great place to stash a box of utility items, such as flashlights,

batteries, replacement light bulbs, a fire extinguisher, candles, matches, and a rope ladder for emergencies.

- ✔ **Shelf 2 (close to eye level):** Upper shelves often don't provide as much height as other shelves, making them ideal for storing flat, stackable items such as tablecloths, table runners, and cloth napkins.

- ✔ **Shelf 3 (chest height):** This is the most convenient shelf to load and unload and as such should hold frequently used items — bed sheets, pillowcases, hand towels, and washcloths.

- ✔ **Shelf 4 (waist height):** Mid-level shelves tend to be spacious and can accommo-date bulky items, such as large bath towels and comforters.

- ✔ **Shelf 5 (lowest shelf):** The lowest shelf is the largest and should be reserved for seasonal items or bulky items — beach towels, holiday linens, heavy blankets, and sleeping bags.

Hanging Whimsical Wall Shelves

Stuff You Need to Know

Toolbox:
- ✔ Measuring tape
- ✔ Pencil
- ✔ Level
- ✔ Drill
- ✔ Drill bits
- ✔ Drywall anchors
- ✔ Screwdriver

Materials:
- ✔ Wall shelves (with mounting hardware)

Time Needed:
Less than an hour

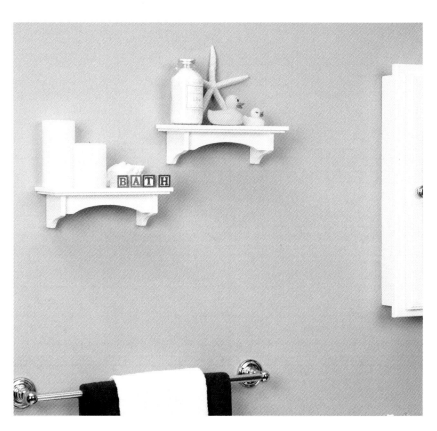

Every room in your home should have a balance of function and fun. Bathrooms tend to be high on the "function" end of the spectrum because they have to store all the items dedicated to health, beauty, and bathing. Often the "fun" gets overlooked! You can carve out a few square feet of "fun" by adding whimsical shelves on your bathroom walls or over the toilet.

Fill up your collection of wall shelves with lightweight fun items that reflect your personality — perhaps ocean-inspired pieces like sea glass, starfish, and driftwood; black-and-white photos of children or grandchildren . . . in the bath (think bubbles!); treasured collections of glass boxes, antiques, and porcelain figurines; or silly items like a collection of rubber ducks.

1 Determine how many shelves you want to hang and the location of your wall shelving. Keep in mind that shelves add visual interest over a towel bar, bath tub, or toilet. If you choose to hang more than one shelf, I recommend purchasing identical shelves for a streamlined look (and to make installation easier).

2

Arrange the grouping of shelves in a formation on the floor in order to help you visualize their design on the wall. If you want to create a staggered effect, measure and write down the vertical and horizontal distance between each shelf (for example, "Shelf 2 is 6 inches down and 4 inches to the left of Shelf 1").

Note: All measurements should be made from the hanging mechanisms of one shelf to the hanging mechanisms of the next in order to tell you where to drill holes for each shelf.

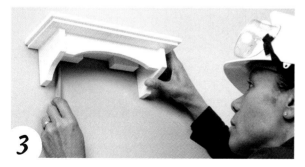

3

Hold the highest shelf in your design up to the wall. Mark the locations of the hanging mechanisms in pencil. (A second pair of hands may come in handy here.)

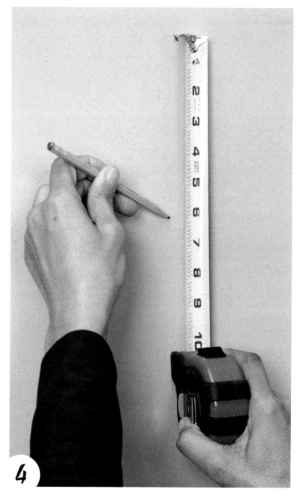

4

Use your measurements from Step 2 to determine where to hang your second shelf. For example, measure 6 inches down and then 4 inches to the left of your marks in Step 3, and mark the spots with a pencil. These spots correspond to the hanging mechanisms of the shelf because they're derived from the hanging mechanisms of the first shelf. Repeat this step for any additional shelves.

Because decorative shelves are generally lightweight and don't hold particularly heavy items, locating a wall stud isn't required for this project.

5

Use a level to double-check all pencil marks for all shelves. Adjust your marks as needed.

6

Using a drill bit with a slightly smaller diameter than the screws required for the hanging mechanism, drill holes in the marked spots for all the shelves by applying consistent horizontal pressure to each hole.

7

Add drywall anchors to each drilled hole to reinforce the strength of the installation. Simply position the drywall anchor in the predrilled hole and tap it with a hammer until the anchor is almost completely in the hole.

8

Use your screwdriver to attach the highest shelf to the wall first. By installing from the top down, lower shelves don't interfere with the installation of higher shelves. Proceed to attach the remaining shelves to the wall.

TIP

If you're crafty, paint or decoupage your shelves before you hang them. Stick with the colors and finishes of your bathroom to unify your decorating scheme!

Installing an Above-the-Toilet Cabinet

Stuff You Need to Know

Toolbox:

- Measuring tape
- Stud finder
- Pencil
- Level
- Drill
- Drill bits
- Screwdriver

Materials:

- Above-the-toilet cabinet (with mounting hardware)

Time Needed:
Less than an hour

Just when you thought you were out of storage space, some innovative soul dreamt up above-the-toilet storage. You wouldn't want a few square feet of perfectly good storage to go to waste, now would you?

Above-the-toilet cabinets, also known as *space savers,* are available in a few different styles. Lightweight shelving supported by four long legs that straddle the toilet tank is often constructed of metal or wicker and requires no installation. Cabinetry supported by four long legs that straddle the toilet tank may require assembly or height adjustment, but otherwise requires no installation.

Then there's wall-mounted cabinetry, which is similar to a wall-mounted kitchen cabinet and provides the most polished look. For ease of installation, choose a cabinet that uses a hanging mechanism (one part affixed to the cabinet slides into another part that you mount on the wall) rather than long screws that you have to drill through the cabinet and into the walls.

1

2

Determine the location of your cabinet. If you're hanging a very shallow cabinet with a depth similar to the toilet tank, hanging it about 6 inches above the tank allows enough space to open the tank, as needed. If you're hanging a deep cabinet, you need to provide some head room so one can easily sit on the toilet underneath the cabinet. In this case, I recommend locating the bottom of your cabinet at least 26 inches above the toilet tank.

Measure your chosen space with a measuring tape to ensure there's enough room.

Measure the distance from the bottom of the cabinet to one of the hanging mechanisms affixed to the back of it.

TIP

Space savers are an excellent solution if you have a pedestal-style sink, which provides limited or no storage space under your bathroom sink.

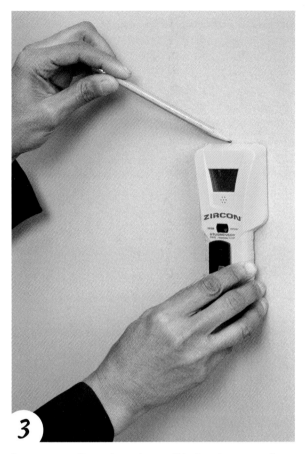

3

Locate a wall stud on the wall behind your toilet with a stud finder, and mark it with pencil. If you're unable to locate a wall stud, add drywall anchors in Step 7 to reinforce the installation.

4

Determine the height at which to drill your holes for the hanging mechanisms by adding the measurements from Steps 1 and 2. Mark this height in pencil where it meets the stud marks from Step 3.

5

Measure the distance between the hanging mechanisms on the back of the cabinet, and transfer this measurement to the wall so you know where to drill your holes.

6

Use a level to verify that the marks from Step 5 are level.

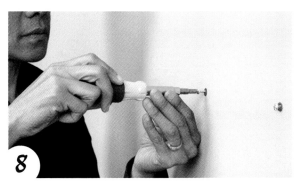

Use a screwdriver to twist the screws into the drilled holes or anchors.

Using a drill bit with a slightly smaller diameter than the screws required for the hanging mechanisms, drill holes in the marked spots, applying consistent horizontal pressure. If your screw holes don't line up with the wall studs marked in Step 3, add drywall anchors to the screw holes by inserting them in the holes and then tapping them almost flush to the wall with a hammer.

Note that heavy-duty wall cabinets don't attach via a hanging mechanism but rather with long screws drilled through the back of the cabinet directly into the wall. If you opt for a cabinet with this type of installation, you definitely need two people to do the job. Using the height determined in Step 1, one person should hold the cabinet up to the wall while the other person ensures that it's level. Drill holes through the back of the cabinet into the wall stud in at least two locations. Insert 3-inch screws through the cabinet into the wall using a screwdriver or drill equipped with a screwdriver head.

Hang your storage cabinet by sliding the hanging mechanisms onto the screws.

Hanging a Medicine Cabinet

How do you *live* in your bathroom? Are you a minimalist with a mirror and pedestal sink? Do you have an oversized vanity and built-ins? Whether you exist simply or robustly in your bathroom, a medicine cabinet is a great organizational addition.

A medicine cabinet has many benefits: It's an additional mirror; generally is moisture resistant (unlike regular cabinets); holds supplies and products; and allows you to conceal countertop toiletries.

1 Determine the location of your medicine cabinet. If your vanity has a wall mirror, locate the cabinet on the nearest side wall. If your medicine cabinet will function as the primary mirror in your bathroom, center it over the vanity. ***Remember:*** Medicine cabinets are very heavy and need to be mounted into wall studs, so the stud location may influence the location of your medicine cabinet.

2

Locate the wall stud in your desired location with a stud finder, and mark it in pencil.

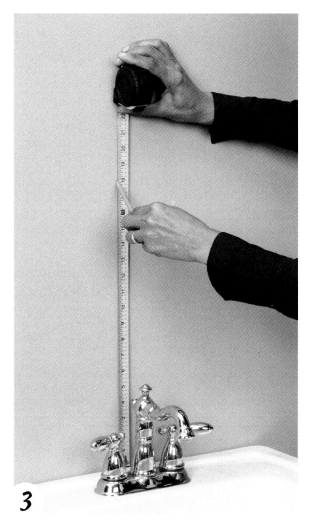

3

With a measuring tape, determine how far above the vanity counter your cabinet will hang. The height of your cabinet needs to accommodate the primary user, whether that be a 4-foot child or a 6-foot adult. Conventional heights are 50 inches from the floor or 18 inches above the countertop. Mark the wall at the bottom of the cabinet height.

If you're having a hard time visualizing the proper height for your cabinet, cut out a piece of newspaper the exact size of the cabinet and tape it to the wall. This template provides a good visual and is easy to adjust and play around with!

TIP

If both you and your significant other use a wide variety of products, consider installing two medicine cabinets to corral countertop clutter like contect lens products and deodorant.

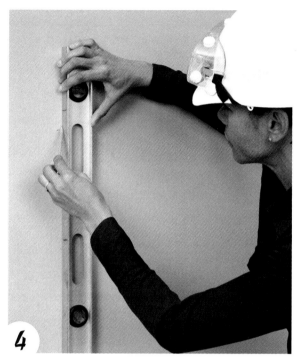

4

Use a level to verify that the pencil marks you made in Steps 2 and 3 are aligned.

5

This installation requires drilling through the back of the medicine cabinet into the wall stud. Use a measuring tape to locate the center of the top of the medicine cabinet. (Note that some medicine cabinets have a reinforced/wood portion at the top, so installing at least one screw through this area is essential.)

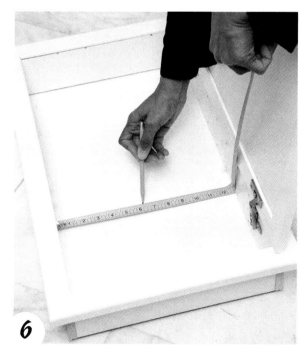

6

Use a measuring tape to locate a few additional horizontally centered spots on the cabinet for drilling.

7

Hold the medicine cabinet up to the wall at the height determined in Step 3, and make sure the marked center of your cabinet lines up with the marked wall stud so that the stud can support the weight of the cabinet. (Note that you may need a helper.)

Using a drill bit with a slightly smaller diameter than the screws required for this installation, drill holes in the marked spots on the cabinet, applying consistent horizontal pressure.

If the holes aren't drilled into wall studs, insert heavy-duty drywall anchors (called *Molly bolts* or *toggle bolts*) to strengthen the installation before you attach the cabinet to the wall. Drill a hole that's big enough for the bolt to fit through, insert the bolt, and trigger it open according to the instructions on the package (sometimes you need a second screwdriver to do this).

8 Screw the cabinet to the wall with a screwdriver.

Grab your passport and go! Building a travel toiletry kit

Recent legislative changes sure have thrown a kink in air travel. If you're a frequent flier who opts to carry your luggage onboard, the following kit is a must! Start with a large, clear cosmetics organizer with multiple compartments. Label the outside with your mailing address (in case your kit is misplaced), and then fill it with the following items:

- **Non-liquid:** Purchase a back-up set of common toiletries: comb, brush, toothbrush, dental floss, tweezers, disposable razors, fingernail clippers, makeup, deodorant, contact lenses, and lens case. Put these items into a single compartment or zippered plastic bag to distinguish them from liquid items.

- **Liquid:** Purchase trial-size versions of toiletries from your local drugstore. Note that the following items must be in containers that hold 3 ounces or less: shampoo, conditioner, lotion, hair spray, lens cleaner, toothpaste, and mouthwash. Leave these liquid items loose in your travel kit. (Another option is to save bottles of hotel shampoo, conditioner, lotion, and body soap. They're almost always under 3 ounces and perfect for a travel kit.)

- **Medical:** A small collection of medicine can cure most travel woes; pack pain reliever, allergy medication, anti-nausea and anti-diarrhea meds, sunscreen, burn relief, bug spray, small bandages, and antibiotic ointment.

- **Other:** If you have room left in your travel toiletry kit, include a generic converter, lint brush, sewing kit, safety pins, ear plugs, and an eye mask.

The Finishing Touches: Reassembling Your Bathroom

After you've installed one, some, or all the projects that appear earlier in this chapter, it's time to put your bathroom back together again. The following sections provide some inspirational ideas for the finishing touches on your new and improved bathroom.

Medications and cleaning supplies sometimes are stored in bathrooms, but they should always be kept out of the reach of children and pets. The moisture in bathrooms can affect the potency of medications, which are better stored elsewhere. I tell you the best ways to store cleaning supplies in your garage in Chapter 11.

Help, my walls are full! Adding a corner storage unit

Bathrooms are crowded places. Between a sink, toilet, shower, towel bar, cabinet, and maybe even a window, you may have run out of wall space! A corner storage unit is a clever solution for adding even more storage. Who uses the corner anyway?

Corner storage units generally include three to five triangular shelves and range in height from 3 to 5 feet. They may require light assembly, but no installation is involved. Decorative bins, baskets, and boxes can neatly hide a multitude of unattractive bathroom items like toilet paper and air freshener. I talk more about these containers in the next section.

Stash, stow, and store: Using decorative baskets, bins, and boxes

Decorative baskets, bins, and boxes are a home organizer's best friend. The right storage container can transform a pile of unsightly clutter into a clever design statement. Use storage containers to conceal your stuff and accessorize your bathroom; here are some tips:

✔ Select a basket, bin, or box that complements your bathroom. Some popular choices are wicker, sea grass, stainless steel, and fabric.

✔ Use an open-top design (meaning no lid) for items that are decorative or need to be easily accessed. For instance, rolled-up hand towels look great in a natural woven basket. Candles and lotions are also visually pleasing on display.

✔ Use a box with a lid to conceal loose, unsightly, or mismatched items. Personal items such as feminine supplies or hair styling tools are well-placed in a box with a lid. Daily toiletries and paper goods can also be stored in a box with a lid.

✔ Store items near the areas they'll be utilized. For example, collections of hand towels should be located near the sink basin, and bath salts should be near the edge of the bath tub.

Keeping your jewelry neat and tangle-free

Conventional jewelry boxes have an inherent design flaw: Valuable necklaces always end up in a big frustrating tangle. I once tried to use a safety pin to untangle the jumble and actually ended up breaking a delicate gold chain. There are better ways to store your jewelry!

- ✔ If you have a recess, alcove, or dressing area in your bathroom, use a petite wall-mounted peg rack to hold long necklaces. (Belt and tie racks are a bit larger, but they work great; see Chapter 6 for more on them.) The necklaces hang vertically, which prevents tangling. Look for a rack with pegs spaced no more than 1 inch apart to maximize the number of necklaces you can fit on it.

- ✔ If you store your jewelry in a wall cabinet, create your own necklace rack by nailing small finishing nails along one interior wall at 1-inch intervals. This solution doesn't use up any of your cabinet's "footprint" because everything's on the wall.

- ✔ If you want to display your jewelry on the vanity, consider a jewelry tree (see Figure 7-1). This item is available at home organization stores and usually stores up to 12 necklaces — each on its own branch.

- ✔ Use a conventional jewelry box to organize smaller items by category — rings in one section, bracelets in another, earrings in a third.

- ✔ To store all the components of a jewelry set (matching necklace, earrings, ring, and bracelet) together, consider using an old baby food jar! It's clear so that you can easily identify the contents, it's a convenient size to hold a few pieces of jewelry, and it's stackable if you decide to use more than one. Works for me!

Figure 7-1: A jewelry tree prevents necklaces from tangling.

Chapter 8

Organized Home Office, Organized Life

Households are busy! Each day brings a new stack of bills, invitations, newspapers, homework, and junk mail. Paperwork piles begin to form, and before long you've lost control of your home office.

Breathe. Inhale. Exhale. You *can* maintain control of your home office by having a well-planned space that acts as one central location for VIP (Very Important Paper). In an organized office, you add items to your family's calendar, you recycle paper, and you maintain your VIP status. This chapter helps you build an organized office, establish filing systems, and anticipate the daily inflow of paper. If you stick to this system, you *can* maintain your VIP status.

The biggest limitation of a home office is space. You may not be able to devote an entire room to a home office, but fear not! Your home office can be as small as a rolling cart tucked away in a hall closet or as extravagant as a dedicated room with a built-in desk! Either way, this chapter helps you establish your home office as a command center from which you run your household.

Before you can put together your home office, you have to take it all apart. Begin by removing everything from your home office. Pull out all your paperwork, files, electronics, memorabilia, coffee mugs, and knickknacks. This crucial step allows you to assess what you have and enables you to quickly eliminate items that don't support your goal or aren't mindful of your office's limitations.

With the contents of your home office laid out before you, it's time to sort! I recommend sorting your office paperwork and accessories into four large containers labeled as follows:

✔ **STAY:** This item is used regularly, is in good condition, and will stay in the home office. Examples of "stay" items are office furniture and VIP. For example, keep documents that you must retain for tax records, medical records, insurance documents, wills or trust, receipts, warranties, lists, calendar items, and gift ideas.

✔ **MOVE:** This item doesn't belong in your home office — return it to its real home! Examples include knickknacks, collectibles, music CDs, DVDs, books, jewelry, and recipes.

✔ **SHARE:** This item is in good condition but hasn't been used in the last year, is a duplicate, or no longer serves the goal. The best thing to do with it is share it! Examples include unused files, an extra chair, old reference manuals, and old office equipment (such as working printers, fax machines, computers, and phones).

✔ **GO:** Trash or recycle it! A majority of the paperwork stored in a home office belongs in this category, such as invitations for past events, paperwork from your child's school that has already been added to the family calendar, fliers, and junk mail. Old computer software, cables, and wires fall in this category, too.

After you determine what's going to stay in your office, select the projects that help you maximize the storage in this space. When you're done, check out the section "The Finishing Touches: Reassembling Your Home Office" at the end of this chapter for ideas on maintaining your home office's organization.

No room for an office? Creating a countertop command center

An office, at its core, is simply a place where VIP (Very Important Paper) is managed. If you live in tight quarters and can't dedicate a whole room to a home office, I recommend transforming a portion of your kitchen countertop into a small office. To function properly, it should have a clear countertop, a quality file, a to-do box, a stationery stash, a household calendar, and a recycle bin (see the later section "Curing clutter with six essential paper stashes"). If you have the space, you can also keep a small box of hostess gifts and gift bags in this area. With proper overhead shelving, these requirements are so minimal that they can be contained in about 24 inches of counter length.

Where should you locate your countertop office? If you live in a spacious, recently built home you may have a counter space designed specifically to be a small work station. If you live in an older home, you have to get creative! Select a location that has a countertop overhang so a chair or stool can be tucked underneath, is as far away as possible from the cook top, and has adequate access to electrical outlets, cable hookups, and phone jacks. If possible, select a spot with an overhead cabinet or room for shelving.

Build the base of your office by tucking a small chair and recycling bin under your counter. Add your office equipment (computer, printer, phone, and fax), basic office accessories (sticky notes, note pads, pens, pencils, tape, scissors, glue, and stapler), and your file.

As for the rest of your key office components, if you have an upper kitchen cabinet over your countertop desk, fill it up! If you don't have any available vertical space, artfully arrange your storage containers (your to-do box, gift box, and stationery stash) by stacking them, if possible. You can also store these items in a lower cabinet if your counter space doesn't have an overhang suitable for a chair. Don't forget to hang your family calendar nearby!

Mounting a Stationery Center

Stuff You Need to Know

Toolbox:
- ✔ Pencil
- ✔ Stud finder
- ✔ Measuring tape
- ✔ Dril
- ✔ Drill bit
- ✔ Screwdriver

Materials:
- ✔ Stationery center (with mounting hardware)

Time Needed:
Less than an hour

Writing letters allows you to convey your thoughts, pass on advice, and reconnect with loved ones. But by the time you assemble your note cards, favorite pen, stamps, and return address labels, wouldn't it have been easier to send an e-mail? Not anymore! A stationery center is a wall-mounted box in or adjacent to your home office that contains all your note cards, envelopes, stamps, return address labels, and pens. Store your address book in your stationery center, too.

Purchase a box to serve as the foundation piece of your stationery center. For this project, I've zeroed in on a large wall-mounted organizer that has slots for stationery and shallow areas for pens, stamps, and labels. Adapt the steps as needed based on your chosen foundation piece.

1 Determine the location of your stationery center. In that area, locate wall studs with a stud finder (see Chapter 2) and mark in pencil. (If you choose to use a lightweight wire file folder for this project, wall stud installation isn't necessary.)

If you plan to hang your organizer on a wall adjacent to your desk, measure the distance between the bottom of the unit and the hanging mechanism on the back of the unit. Add 12 inches to this measurement to determine the height at which you will hang your stationery center above your desktop. Measure and mark the wall stud with a pencil at this height.

If you plan to hang your organizer in a space that isn't adjacent to your desk, aim to install the top of the stationery center at eye level. (Your eye-level height is about 3 inches less than your height.) Because the hanging mechanism for this type of product tends to be located at the top of the unit, no further measuring is necessary. Mark the wall stud with a pencil at this height.

If the hanging mechanism detaches from the unit, remove it and hold it against the wall at the height determined in Step 2. If you're not able to detach it, hold the entire unit up to the wall at the height determined in Step 2. Push your pencil through the screw holes on the hanging mechanism to indicate where you'll drill your holes.

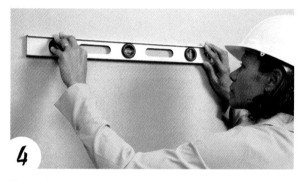

If you have more than one pencil mark for the hanging mechanism, use your level to ensure that they're level.

TIP

A medicine cabinet with adjustable shelves is a clever solution for a stationery center and is available in a wide variety of materials and colors. Just be sure to pick one that's deep enough to hold all your stationery! Turn to Chapter 7 for instructions on installing a medicine cabinet. Other options include wall-mounted file holders, wall cubbies, organizational units, and wall pockets.

5

Using a drill bit with a slightly smaller diameter than the screws required for the hanging mechanism, drill holes in all marked spots, applying consistent horizontal pressure.

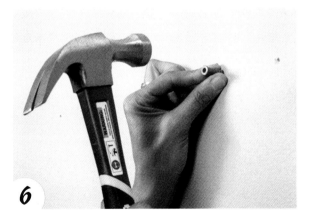

6

If you're not drilling into wall studs, reinforce the installation by using drywall anchors. Simply position the drywall anchor in the predrilled hole and tap with a hammer until the anchor is almost completely in the hole.

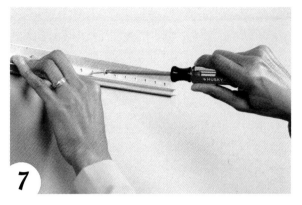

7

Screw the hanging mechanism onto the wall using a screwdriver.

8

Hang your stationery center by sliding or angling the unit on the hanging mechanism bracket.

TIP

Load up your stationery center with all the items required to write a heartfelt note: thank you notes, blank note cards, monogrammed stationery, and envelopes of various sizes. Tuck loose items like stamps and return address labels into blank envelopes or small boxes. Store pens in a small cup or container, just like you would store your toothbrush in your medicine cabinet! To make stacking easier, keep stationery in the original boxes if your stationery center is large enough to accommodate them. Grab a photo from your nearby photo box and enclose it with your letter to give it a personal touch.

Building a Homemade Desk

If you're short on cash or just starting out in an apartment or dorm, this is the project for you! You take common household items and combine them to make a functional desk. Quick, cheap, and easy — that's my kind of project!

Begin by determining the height of your workspace. Sit in your office chair with your feet firmly planted on the ground. Extend your arms straight out in front of you. Your desk should be about 2 inches lower than your arm height and several inches above your knee height. While sitting, use a measuring tape extended up from the floor to get a precise height.

You can use a variety of items as the base of your desk. Select a pair of items that have a flat, level surface and are in your comfortable height range. Two wood or metal filing cabinets of the same height (usually around 30 inches) work great and provide plenty of file storage as a bonus. Sturdy stainless-steel trash cans give a contemporary look to a loft or artsy space. A set of nightstands work if they're the right height. Stacks of cinder blocks and plastic crates (weighted down, of course) are other very inexpensive options.

Select a flat, rectangular surface to use as the top of your desk. A door is extremely sturdy and provides ample desk space; just be sure to use one without recessed panels.

For this project, I've zeroed in on a homemade desk made from two metal filing cabinets and a solid-surface door. Adapt the steps as needed based on your chosen materials.

1

Lay the door flat on the floor (protected by a dropcloth), on sawhorses, or on chairs draped with dropcloths.

2

If you've purchased a new door for this project, move on to the next step. If you're repurposing a door to serve as the top of your desk, remove all hardware (hinges, knobs, and stoppers) with a screwdriver. Wipe down the door with clean rags and a soap and water solution to remove dirt, grease, and oils. Let the door dry completely before moving on.

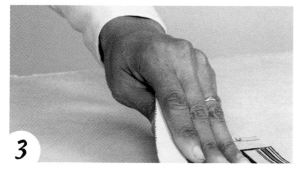

3

Sand the door with medium-grit sandpaper to remove any splinters or rough patches. Then wipe it down with a damp cloth to remove dust.

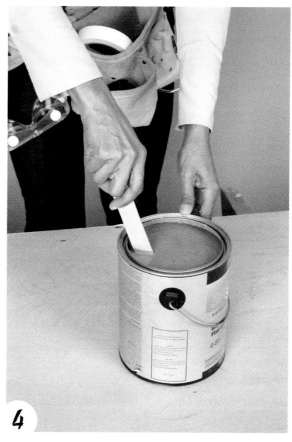

4

Stir your paint or wood stain thoroughly with a stir stick. If you're using a roller to apply paint or stain to the door, pour some from the can into a paint tray.

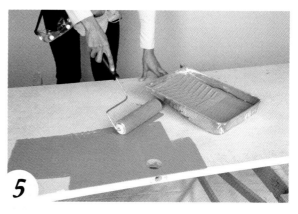

5

Paint or stain both sides of the door, following the manufacturer's instructions. Use long, continuous strokes for the best results.

6 Let the paint or stain dry according to the manufacturer's instructions. If you stained the door, consider repeating Steps 3 through 5 with polyurethane to protect and seal the finish. (Follow the polyurethane manufacturer's instructions for application.)

Set the door on the filing cabinets. If the door has a doorknob hole, position that at the back of the desktop (opposite where you'll sit) and use it as a pass-through for computer cords, power cords, and phone lines. A door is heavy enough not to shift on the base, so no further installation is necessary.

To secure a lighter desktop material like plywood to a dissimilar surface such as metal, you can glue the top to the base. Select glue that's appropriate for both the top surface and the bottom surface. (The salespeople at your local home improvement store should be able to steer you in the right direction.) If you're connecting a plywood top to wood filing cabinets, you can nail the two together with either a hammer or a nail gun — use a nail at each corner and at 6- to 12-inch intervals wherever the plywood intersects the cabinet. Remember to always wear safety goggles when using a nail gun.

If you don't want a piece of wood as your desktop, a sheet of glass (regular or tempered) provides a contemporary look. (Note that glass corners are very sharp and should be professionally rounded or beveled.) A sheet of glass is generally heavy enough to stay in place, but if you're worried about shifting, consider adding a bit of putty adhesive at each corner.

Use your measuring tape to determine the length of the door. Transfer this measurement to the floor of your home office by placing a piece of masking tape at each end of the length. Position your two filing cabinets so that the outside edge of each cabinet lines up with the masking tape. Remove the masking tape.

Creating a Home Office Space

If you don't have a whole room to devote to a home office, why not make great use of empty space within a room? It should be at least 36 inches wide and 20 inches deep, have adequate wall space and ceiling height to add shelving, and have an accessible electrical outlet and phone jack (if your components aren't wireless). Additionally, the office shouldn't detract from the function of the room or space around it.

Measure the height, width, and depth of your space. If you're using a desk or desk/hutch combination, select the desk with the largest possible width that will fit. For instance, if your space measures 48½ inches wide, buy a desk up to 48 inches wide. If you're purchasing a piece of plywood to serve as a top on a homemade desk (see the previous project), have the plywood cut to ½ inch less than both the width and depth of the space to account for walls that aren't exactly square.

If you've purchased or created a flat desk, you need shelving! I recommend purchasing several floating wooden wall shelves that are slightly smaller than the width of your space and less than half as deep. For example, if your space is 48½ inches wide and 28½ inches deep, select shelving that's about 48 inches wide and less than 14 inches deep.

The first shelf should be slightly higher than the computer on your desktop. Plan subsequent shelves at different height levels, keeping in mind the height of your space and how you plan to use your shelves. No matter how you plan to use your shelves, make a list of the shelf heights for your project as measured from the desktop height, not the floor. For example, the shelving in this project is at heights of 24, 32, and 42 inches above the desktop.

It's easier to hang shelving above a desk if the desk is out of the way, so use a pencil to mark the height of your desk along the wall in your space. Then temporarily move the desk out of the space.

Locate the wall studs in the back of the space with a stud finder (see Chapter 2) and mark them with a pencil.

Determine the location of the first, highest shelf according to your game plan; in this project, that's 42 inches above the desktop. Use your measuring tape to measure this distance along the wall stud, and mark this height.

Detach the hanging mechanism from your first wall shelf. Align the hanging mechanism with the mark from Step 3. Use a pencil to mark through the screw holes so you know where to drill.

5

Use a level to ensure that the pencil marks are level.

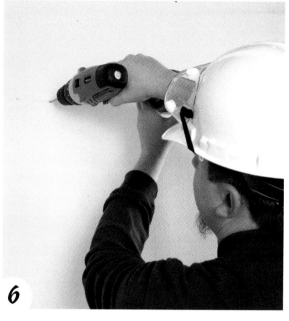

6

Using a drill bit with a slightly smaller diameter than the screws required for the hanging mechanism, drill holes in the marked spots, applying consistent horizontal pressure.

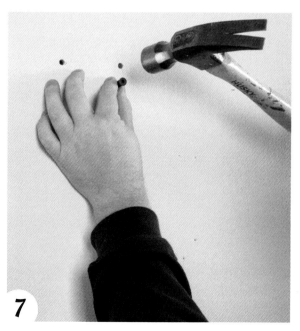

7

If any of the holes aren't drilled into wall studs, add drywall anchors to them to reinforce this installation. Simply position the drywall anchor into the hole and tap it with a hammer until the anchor is almost completely in the hole.

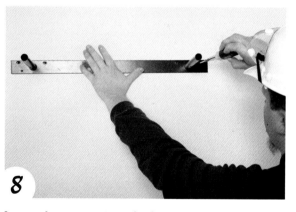

8

Insert the screws into the hanging mechanism, and use your screwdriver to screw it in place.

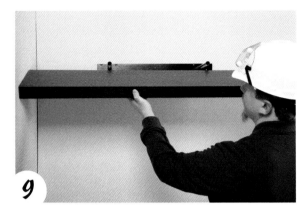

9

Hang your floating wall shelf by angling or sliding the shelf onto the attached hanging mechanism. Every shelf is different; if necessary connect the shelf to the hanging mechanism with small screws provided with the shelf.

10 Repeat this process for additional shelves at the heights you determined in your game plan, working down from the highest shelf to the lowest.

11 Replace your desk in the space, and outfit your new home office with your computer, printer, office supplies, and other essentials.

An alternative to a desk: An office on wheels

If you live in very tight quarters, you'll really appreciate this idea! If you don't have the space to dedicate to a conventional home office, you can create a *mobile* home office. When not in use, you roll your mobile home office into a hallway closet, spare bedroom, or underneath a staircase. If you don't have an alternative storage space, you can conceal the whole lot with a custom fabric or leather cover.

Decide what you plan to store in your mobile home office. Items include office machines (laptop and printer), supplies, accessories (sticky notes, note pads, pens, pencils, tape, scissors, glue, and stapler), files, and boxes.

Estimate the number of levels you'll need and the location of each item. I recommend storing your laptop on the top level, the printer and its supplies on the second level, your file and to-do box on the third level, and any overflow of items on the bottom level. If you have room, you can also store your gift box and stationery stash on the rolling cart. (See the later section "Curing clutter with six essential paper stashes" for more about these items.)

Purchase a rolling cart from a large home store or office supply store that has enough tiers to accommodate your needs. If you're going to store only one piece of office equipment (your laptop computer, for example), select a three-tier cart; if you're going to store multiple pieces of electronics (your computer, printer, and fax machine or scanner), you'll probably need a four-tier cart. Whatever the size, select a cart constructed from a sturdy material (like stainless steel or wire) with a lip on each tray so items don't slip off during transport.

A key step of building your mobile home office is properly harnessing all power cords and wires into a single surge protector. *Remember that surge protectors are a must when using computers or other office equipment.* Attach a surge protector to the lowest level of the cart using zip ties or wire or heavy-duty twist ties (see the later section "Taking charge of cords" for details on these items). Thread all electronics cords through the rear of the shelves to the surge protector, and plug them in. Gather any excess cord length and secure it to itself and then to the cart with zip ties, rubber bands, or twist ties.

The Finishing Touches: Reassembling Your Home Office

After you've installed one, some, or all the projects that appear in this chapter, it's time to take your home office to the next level. The following sections provides some inspirational ideas for enhancing your command center.

Lining up electronic equipment

Are you inexplicably drawn to the latest and greatest electronic gizmos? You're not alone! Many people are quick to buy electronics — beyond computers — that scan, print, fax, laminate, store, and automate all the bits of information in life. After you've weeded out any unnecessary items (see the beginning of this chapter), it's time to find a home for everything that must stay. Here are some tips for doing just that:

- Locate your computer monitor (and desktop PC, if that's what you have) in the rear of your desktop, directly in front of your chair. Positioning your computer as far back as possible gives you extra workspace in the front of the desk area. (A keyboard and mouse are easy to move out of the way to clear space to work when you're not using the computer.) The area behind your computer is unusable space anyway.

- Electronics that require top-loading (some printers, scanners, and faxes) need to be located on a desktop or a shelf with enough clearance to allow you to access the top.

- Electronics that have a front-loading feature (some printers and faxes) may be stacked, either on your desktop or on shelves, to clear up valuable desk space.

- Corral small items, like digital camera equipment, cables, and chargers, into a small decorative box, and store it on a shelf above or near your computer.

- Store infrequently used electronics like laminators or label-makers underneath your desk or on an upper shelf.

Taking charge of cords

It's simple to arrange your office equipment: The computer goes here, and the printer goes there. Arranging the cords, wires, and cables is a whole different story! One way to avoid a tangle of cords is to purchase wireless office equipment. Wireless devices communicate by electromagnetic waves in lieu of wires, cords, and cables. Printers, fax machines, keyboards, mice, and network routers are all available in wireless formats.

If you're currently committed to office equipment with cords, endless innovations are available to help you deal with the tangles. After you have your office equipment configured to your liking, plug all cords and chargers into the surge protector. Gather the excess length of cord into a tight bundle, and bind it with one of the following:

- ✔ **Cable tie or twister:** Similar to a garbage bag twister, you wrap the cable twister around a folded-up bundle of excess cord length to make a tight grouping. This binder is available in plastic, wire, and even Velcro (see Figure 8-1).

- ✔ **Cable zipper or snake:** String several full-length cords through a rigid cable zipper, fabric sleeve, or coil to enclose them in a single tube (see Figure 8-1).

- ✔ **Charging station:** You plug cellphones, MP3 players, cameras, and other rechargeable devices into the strip in the charging station. The station makes for a tasteful, organized display of gadgets (see Figure 8-2).

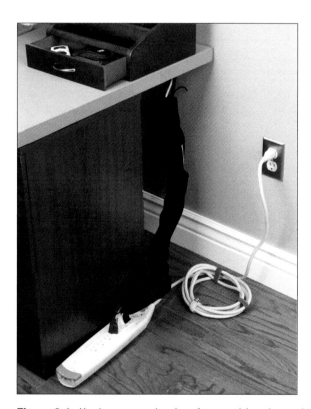

Figure 8-1: You have several options for organizing electronic equipment wires.

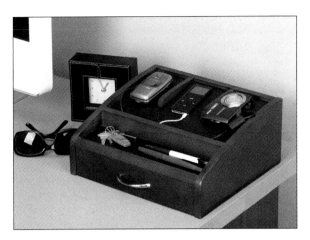

Figure 8-2: You can charge several electronic gadgets in one spot.

Storing small supplies

Every workspace needs basic office supplies like pens, pencils, staples, tacks, brads, erasers, tape, and paperclips. And if you do arts and crafts in your office, the list will include decorative hole punches, colored pens, stickers, and paper cutters. And a calculator for bill paying. And ink cartridges for your printer. And the list goes on! Here are a few clever solutions for organizing small items:

- ✔ **Use a junk drawer organizer.** These handy devices fit into a desk drawer and divide the space into small compartments. The compartments in varying sizes are perfect for storing small items like paperclips, staples, tacks, rubber bands, and binder clips.

- ✔ **Use magnetic spice canisters.** Although they're designed to hold spices, these are the perfect size to hold small office supplies. To free up space both in your drawers and on your desktop, you can adhere the canisters to the magnetic portion of a message board or to a wall-mounted magnetic strip, which is usually included with the canisters.

- ✔ **Store your office tools and accessories on a wall-mounted pegboard.** These boards were designed to hold tools like hammers and screwdrivers in a garage or tool shed, but they're well suited for office tools like rulers, staplers, glue guns, and craft tools. (See Chapter 11 for steps on mounting a pegboard.)

- ✔ **Purchase a small desktop organizer or cosmetics organizer if you don't have an available drawer or wall space.** These organizers hold pens, pencils, rulers, and staplers vertically in compartments. They usually also have small compartments for erasers, tape, and paperclips, too!

- ✔ **When in doubt, display your pens and pencils in a decorative mug or bud vase.** Remember, less is more!

Curing clutter with six essential paper stashes

In this chapter, one of your goals is to make your home office an organized central location for all your VIP (Very Important Paper). A vital part of meeting this goal is to route all incoming paperwork to its respective location! The following six prescriptions should help you cure your cluttered office:

✔ **File:** If you've already taken action on an item, file it! Your file is the most frequently used component on your desk, so select one with a sturdy construction and an appealing look! I recommend a vertical file box or an accordion file with at least 13 sections — sufficient to accommodate the main household categories discussed in the next section. Keep your file on a shelf in your home office that you can access while seated. The easier it is to access, the more likely you are to maintain a tidy workspace.

✔ **To-do box:** As you sort through your daily inflow of paperwork, anything that you need to take action on should be routed to your to-do box. Examples are bills to pay, invitations to RSVP for, and school permission slips to sign. Because you'll use this box daily (I certainly do), I recommend a sturdy, attractive box with an open top. Stow this box in the most convenient spot possible, at arm's length. It's important that you review the contents of this box frequently — at least weekly.

✔ **Gift box:** A gift box that contains small gifts you plan to give in the future (such as hostess gifts), inspirations for gifts pulled from magazines, and a year-round holiday gift list saves so much rushing around time! Your gift box should be a medium-size container with a lid. ***Remember:*** This is *not* the place to stash your trove of holiday gifts! If you have the room, store your gift box on the highest shelf or least accessible area within your home office. If you don't have the space, this box can be stored in an alternative location, like a hall closet or garage.

Be clever! If you find a hostess gift that's a hit, buy several to keep on hand for future events. If you see an age-appropriate toy for your children that's on sale, buy a few for their friends' birthdays. If your favorite bottle of wine goes on sale, buy a few extra bottles to bring to holiday parties. Candles, potpourri, and cookbooks are also easy yet thoughtful hostess gifts.

If you plan to wrap gifts at your desk, store the following items in the gift box as well: small, neutral-colored gift bags; colored tissue paper; gift tabs; ribbons and bows; tape; and scissors.

✔ **Stationery stash:** Everyone enjoys receiving handwritten notes, but does everyone love to write them? Having everything you need in one box makes letter writing less of a burden. If you don't have a wall-mounted stationery center (see the project earlier in this chapter), fill a medium box with thank you notes, blank note cards, plain and decorative stationery, envelopes, stamps, return address labels, pens, and your address book. You can also include duplicate or extra photos or pressed flowers with your correspondence (but don't keep photos in this box indefinitely; they belong in albums or designated photo boxes).

✔ **Family calendar:** A calendar is essential for every well-run household! I recommend using the available calendar option on your computer or a calendar available through your e-mail provider. I like online calendars because events are easily changed or deleted (rather than crossed out and rewritten), and you can add items as recurring events, such as birthdays (annual) or exercise classes (every Wednesday). You can print out electronic calendars weekly or monthly to suit your needs.

✔ **Recycle bin:** Home offices are full of paperwork, and most of it should be directed to your recycle bin. Tackle a paper task, and move on! In order to protect against identity theft, all personal or financial information (essentially anything with your name, social security number, address, phone number, medical information, or an account number) should be cross-cut shredded and then recycled.

What's missing? Lists! Store your lists — grocery, home improvement, gift, and so on — adjacent to your family calendar or message center. This location ensures that each event on the calendar results in a corresponding item added to a list; for example, the calendar event "Family Secret Santa Exchange" prompts you to add "$30 gift for Cousin Erik" to the gift list. Chapter 5 tells you how to install a message center.

Filing your most important papers

First and foremost, a filing system needs to be large enough to accommodate your VIP (Very Important Paper). Each household will have a different definition of VIP, but generally it includes information on taxes, bills, medical records, household items, and insurance documents.

Portable file boxes, filing cabinets, and accordion files are all great options for filing systems; choose the one that suits your needs and your available office space. You also have plenty of labeling options: Home office stores sell labels in many styles (clear, white, and colored) and sizes. You can handwrite your labels or print directly onto labels using your printer. Keep in mind that your filing system will be a permanent fixture on or near your desk and used frequently, so you should like the way it looks and feels!

Accordion files generally have 13 sections, and you can expand portable file boxes and file cabinets to more than 13 sections. Whichever you use, I recommend dividing your filing system into the following categories:

✔ Medical

✔ Bills

✔ Current warranties

✔ Phone lists

✔ Travel

✔ Gift certificates/coupons

- ✔ Work documents
- ✔ Insurance documents
- ✔ Copy of wills/trust
- ✔ School records
- ✔ Tax receipts for the current year
- ✔ Bank statements for the current year
- ✔ Sentimental items

You can keep past tax receipts and bank statements, up to seven years past, in a long-term storage area like the garage, attic, or basement.

Staying on top of incoming papers

You've probably heard someone say he's "trying to climb out from underneath a mountain of paperwork." If you don't stay on top of your incoming paperwork — namely magazines, invitations, and bills — it doesn't seem like such an exaggeration. Follow these helpful tips to keep your small stack of paper from turning into a mountain:

- ✔ **Magazines:** Beautiful, glossy magazines are very alluring! They're a great source of inspiration for exercise, lifestyle, menu planning, and fashion. If you come across an inspiring item, tear it out of the magazine (really!) and then put it in your file if you must keep it, your to-do box if you're going to take action on it, or your gift box if it's inspiration for a gift.

  If you find that you aren't able to read your current issue before the next issue arrives, then cancel your subscription! Eliminating magazine subscriptions is good for both the environment and your pocketbook! You also can consider transferring your subscription to a local women's shelter, senior center, or library.

- ✔ **Invitations:** An active social calendar makes it a challenge to keep up with the constant barrage of invitations. Invitations no longer just come in your mailbox but also via e-mail, phone call, and Internet! With all the different avenues of receiving invitations, it's easy to overlook RSVP'ing to an event or forgetting an event that you have already RSVP'd for. (Cringe!)

  To alleviate this unfortunate situation, stick to the following key steps:

  1. **RSVP to the event in a timely and appropriate manner. E-mail is fastest — but obviously not appropriate for a wedding!**

  2. **Add the event, the address of the event, and any food to bring (for potluck events) to the household calendar.**

  3. **Add any gifts required to your to-do or shopping list.**

  4. **Add any food to bring (for potluck events) to your grocery list.**

  5. **Program the phone number and address of the location of the event into your cellphone or add them to your day planner (an item that you carry with you daily).**

  6. **Toss the invite in the recycle bin if it's the old-fashioned kind.**

✔ **Bills:** It's no fun to eat Chinese takeout food in the dark. Well, maybe it's a little fun, but it's not something you want to make a habit of. Bills should be dealt with in a consistent and methodic manner to ensure that your electricity and other utilities and services never get turned off! Handle incoming bills in the following manner:

1. **Open the bill and shred/recycle the envelope.**

2. **Highlight the due date of the bill.**

3. **Add the bill to your to-do box.**

4. **Designate one day a week as the day to pay all household bills . . . perhaps "Money Monday"!**

5. **Add "Money Monday" as a weekly recurring event on your calendar so that you're prompted to pay bills each week.**

Bills almost always give you at least seven days between when the bill arrives and when payment is actually due. If you pay all your bills on the same day every week, they'll never be late! Additionally, almost every bill can be paid online, which saves a stamp and mailing time. Many bills are the same amount every month (like a cable bill or gym membership) and can be set up under an auto-pay option so that payment is automatically deducted from your account on a set date each month. Isn't technology great?

Putting together a totally to-date tax record tower

It's hard to be an adult! Every April 15, you're expected to submit your federal and state tax records from the previous year. This means that from January 1 through December 31, you need to keep all items pertinent to your tax returns, especially

✔ Receipts

✔ Cancelled checks

✔ Proof of payments

✔ Income statements

✔ Investment records

✔ Bank statements

✔ Deductions

And after April 15, you're expected to keep this entire collection of tax records for years! And it needs to be labeled and accessible! It may sound like a daunting task, but there's a good solution: a tax tower! A tax tower is a vertical storage tower located within your home office that's constructed of seven stackable boxes. Select boxes that are large enough to hold your tax records for an entire year, have reinforced edges, and are strong enough to stack seven high. A sturdy hat box is perfectly suited for this project.

Each box contains an entire year's worth of tax records. For 364 days of the year this tower looks like a narrow file cabinet or column in the corner of your home office. The top level of the tower can be dressed up with a lightweight table lamp, picture frame, or vase.

On Tax Day, you remove the table lamp and take apart the tower. The bottom level (tax records from seven years ago) is emptied and refilled with the current year's tax records. This box is relabeled with the current year and placed on top! Replace your table lamp or decoration, and you're prepared should the IRS come calling. (Cross your fingers that they don't.)

Tax records — which include receipts, W-2s, bank statements, and other financial documentation — need to be kept for at least seven years. Many experts recommend keeping your tax returns (the actual filed documents) indefinitely. When it's time to get rid of the old box of tax records, transfer your returns to long-term storage, and use a cross-cut paper shredder to ensure that all financial information is sufficiently destroyed. Shredded paper bits can be recycled or used for packing material or children's art projects!

Part III
Organizing Secondary Spaces in Your Home

The 5th Wave   By Rich Tennant

In this part . . .

This part addresses the smaller — yet critical — areas of your life at home. These aren't the rooms your family spends much time in, per se, but they are used on a daily basis. Like Part II, this part guides you through the five-step process of home organization, and I provide numerous project suggestions. These chapters are heavy on finishing touches so you can enhance the quality of the time you do spend in your kids' spaces, laundry room, or garage.

Chapter 9

Playing Up Kids' Spaces

Childhood is a magical time for learning, development, and fun. The goal of a kids' space (either a bedroom or a playroom) is an organized room to help your kids do things themselves — and have fun doing it! Features are plenty of space to play and create and accessible storage for stuffed animals, toys, clothing, and linens. Often it's just quicker to do it *yourself,* but in the long run, it pays off to equip children with the skills to do it *themselves* at an early age.

What's the best way to achieve your goal of an organized kids' space? Begin by evaluating your child's bedroom or playroom to determine the limitations of the space. A simple way to accomplish this is to ask yourself the following questions:

✔ Does the closet provide adequate storage?

✔ Is there enough play space in the room?

✔ Does your child have somewhere to work on homework, puzzles, art, and more?

✔ Are piles of toys becoming a problem?

✔ Are you utilizing your wall space for storage solutions?

✔ Have your child's belongings crept into other areas of your home?

The answers to these questions will help you understand the current limitations of your kids' space and decide which projects and finishing touches in this chapter will help you reach your goal.

After you've established a goal and limitations for your kids' space, it's time to sort. Review your children's belongings (clothing, toys, and books) and sort the items into four categories: STAY, MOVE, SHARE, and GO. This crucial step will help you determine what volume of stuff needs to be stored and establish specific requirements for your projects — you can't hang a stuffed animal net until you know how many stuffed animals it needs to hold!

- ✔ **STAY:** This item is in good condition, is used often, is relevant to the goal, and will stay in the room. Examples include clothing that's in good shape and regularly worn and toys and books that are in good shape, age appropriate, and used often.

- ✔ **MOVE:** This item is in good condition and used often, but it doesn't belong in the kids' space. Who knows what items kids will drag into their room next! When you're sorting through your children's space, you're likely to find random items like scuba equipment, dusters, or Mommy's high heels that have been missing for months!

- ✔ **SHARE:** This item is in good condition but hasn't been used in the last year, is a duplicate, or no longer serves the goal of the room. Examples include excess stuffed animals and furniture, books, clothing, and toys your children have outgrown. If you have younger children (or plan to), move these items to a labeled box in your garage or spare closet until the next one is ready for them.

- ✔ **GO:** This item is trash! Examples include broken toys, worn-out clothing, and torn books.

Encourage your kids to help you sort! Talk to them about the value of donating gently used clothing and toys to families who can't afford to buy their own. Give them an age-appropriate task like sorting through clothing or books, but be careful about asking them to sort through toys or stuffed animals — they'll want to keep all of them!

After you sort the contents of your kids' space, choose the projects that will help you store what's in the "STAY" pile, and get to work! When you're done, check out the section "The Finishing Touches: Reassembling Your Kids' Space" at the end of this chapter for ideas and clever purchases to enhance your children's rooms.

Memory maker: Creating a keepsake box

Phew. Raising kids is definitely a full-time job, and managing the inflow of stuff is certainly a large chunk of it. Every day brings a new delivery of homework, report cards, awards, crafts, photos, goody bags, and gifts. Luckily, most of this stuff is temporary and can be tossed or donated when your child is looking the other way.

Breathe easy knowing that the few items that make the cut can be preserved in a keepsake box. It doesn't have to be pretty; it just has to be large, have a lid, and be waterproof. I recommend using a solid-colored sturdy plastic box because if the box is clear, little eyes may catch sight of a special something and prompt some digging through the contents. Trust me on this one!

Create one keepsake box per child and store it away from little eyes, either in the garage or on an upper shelf in the child's closet. Label the lid with the child's name, and use this box to preserve special items such as

✔ **Precious baby clothes:** Select two to three of your favorite baby outfits or shoes. Make sure each item is properly cleaned before storing it in your keepsake box. You can further preserve the items by storing them in plastic zippered bags. Throw in a fresh baby diaper, too — as the years pass, you'll forget how little those things are!

✔ **Awards:** A title like "Kindergartener of the Month" is quite the honor, and the accompanying certificate should definitely be stored in your child's keepsake box. But you don't need to keep every participation certificate from soccer, gymnastics, or art class. Remember that less is more.

✔ **Professional photographs:** Class photos, school photos, and team photos are great fun to look at years down the road. Remember your own third grade photo with no front teeth? Photographs don't take up much space, so store away! Just be sure to put them into acid-free sleeves and folders to protect them over the years.

✔ **Special creations:** Every now and then, a piece of your child's artwork just melts your heart. Maybe it was your kindergartener trying to paint a family portrait, a really special class project, or the first time your youngster wrote his own name. As artwork and projects pass through your fingertips daily, weed out the really special ones and add them to the keepsake box. Remember, your kids bring home special memories year after year, so limit yourself to no more than 12 pieces a year. You can do it!

✔ **Medals and trophies:** Kids love the validation of receiving trophies or medals for their accomplishments! Embrace this enthusiasm by displaying their accomplishments in their bedrooms. When they tire of having them on display, photograph your child holding each medal or trophy and donate the bulky items to your local Special Olympics or youth sports organization. Many sports leagues recycle old trophies. Keep the photos of the medals or trophies, along with one or two special awards, in your child's keepsake box.

✔ **Written memories:** Childhood passes by in a flurry of activity. If you can, take the time to jot down funny anecdotes, firsts, and reflections in a journal or on note cards. These don't need to be fancy, just heartfelt. Don't forget to add the date of each entry! Store your memory journal in the keepsake box and smile when you stumble upon it ten years later.

You may want to present this keepsake box to your child as a wedding present or housewarming gift. I can think of no better present from a parent to a child.

Hanging a Wall-Mounted Storage Net

Children are drawn to little stuffed animals, medium-sized stuffed animals, and ENORMOUS stuffed animals. A catchall net is the perfect corner-mounted solution that gets stuffed animals off the floor. Assess your child's collection to determine if you need one net or two . . . or six. Storage nets are hung from three hooks in the corner of a room. I recommend hanging your net at a kid-friendly height of 40 to 50 inches off the floor so they can put items away themselves. If you need more than one net, place the lowest net at 36 inches and then hang each additional net above in 24- to 36-inch increments.

1 Use a measuring tape and pencil to mark the height at which you want to hang your net. Mark the corner as well as the two adjacent walls.

2 Using a drill bit that's slightly smaller than the hook required for the net, drill a hole in the corner at the height marked in Step 1, applying consistent horizontal pressure.

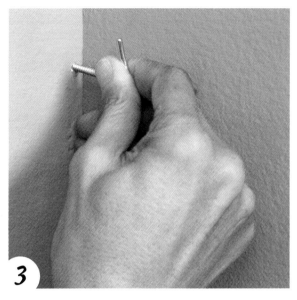

3 Twist a sturdy hook into the corner (as close as possible to the corner) at your chosen height.

4 Hang your net from the corner hook, and stretch it out toward the side walls. Mark the exact locations of your other two hooks with a pencil, noting that the net should be loose enough to cradle a large stuffed animal.

Note: You may want to get some help with this step. It's much easier to measure the proper height and adjust the hooks with two people involved.

6 Using a drill bit that's slightly smaller than the hooks required for the net, drill holes at the spots marked in Step 4, applying consistent horizontal pressure. Screw in the two remaining hooks, and hang your net. Hang additional nets above the first net as desired.

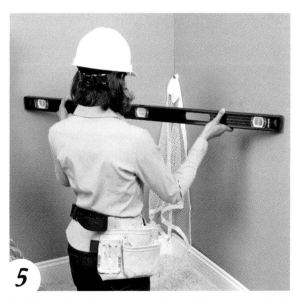

5 Hold your level up against the wall to ensure that each side hook mark is at the same height as the installed corner hook.

TIP

A net works especially well if you have a pet that has mistaken a cherished stuffed animal for a chew toy. Wall-mounted catchall nets also work great for decorative throw pillows!

Customizing a Toy Chest

Stuff You Need to Know

Toolbox:
- Dropcloths or newspaper
- Medium-grit sandpaper
- Clean rags
- Stir sticks for paint
- Paint tray
- Paintbrush or small roller
- Measuring tape
- Disposable plastic plates
- Stencil brushes (one for each accent color)
- Paper towels
- Small paintbrush for detail work

Materials:
- Unfinished wood toy chest
- 1-inch blue painter's tape
- Latex paint in base color
- Stencils (as many as desired)
- Acrylic paints in accent colors for stencils

Time Needed:
About a day

I'm a sucker for theme rooms. In the last few years, I've transformed my daughter's room from garden to rock star to hippie-chick and my son's room from transportation to surfer to jungle. And I think they're both ready for a new transformation! At least I am. . . .

You may not change your room themes quite as often as I do, but I'm certain you can identify the decorating style, theme, or color scheme of your child's room. This project tells you how to transform an unfinished wood box into a designer storage accessory, complete with stenciled images and your child's name (or a special message), that coordinates with your child's room.

I recommend selecting an unfinished toy chest with safety hinges that prevent the lid from slamming closed on little fingers. Toy chests are great storage solutions for bulky stuffed animals or dress-up clothes, so buy a roomy one (at least 32 inches wide).

Adorn your child's toy chest with unexpected theme elements to add even more punch. For example, for a pirate theme, hot glue a few gold coins on the chest. For a princess theme, attach a princess tiara, earrings, and a feather boa border to the chest. Let your imagination run wild!

1

Prepare a well-ventilated painting area by laying down dropcloths or newspaper to protect the floor. Cover the hinges and any other hardware on the toy chest with blue painter's tape to protect it from paint.

2

Sand the chest with medium-grit sandpaper to eliminate splinters and smooth the surface. Wipe it down with a clean, damp rag to remove dust for a paint-ready surface.

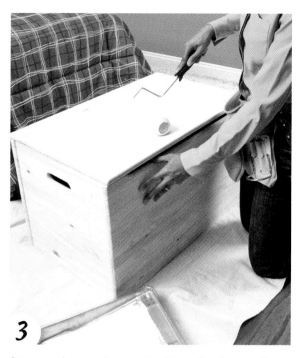

3

Stir your base color paint with a stir stick, and then pour some into a paint tray (it's more manageable than painting directly from the can). Using a paintbrush or small roller, paint your toy chest a light base color, such as white, cream, light blue, or light pink so that darker-colored stencils will pop. If you plan to use very dark accent stencils, you may opt for a deeper base color, like gray.

Note: Let the base coat of paint dry completely before you move on to stenciling.

4

Place the first stencil where you want it on the toy chest, and use a measuring tape to ensure that it's centered. Use painter's tape to secure the stencil.

5

Shake up the stencil paints, and squirt a small amount of each onto the plastic plates.

6

Load a stencil brush with paint by gently dipping the tips of the brush in the paint. Blot off excess paint by tapping the bristle tips on a paper towel. The brush should look almost dry before you apply it to the stencil.

7

Lightly pounce color onto select areas of the stencil and toy chest by quickly touching the brush bristles to the stencil and pulling the brush straight up and away.

8

Repeat Steps 4 through 7 for additional stencils until you've achieved your desired look. If you plan to use a stencil with multiple colors, let the first color of paint fully dry before overlapping a new color.

9

After all paint has completely dried, use a small brush to outline your figures or add extra decorative touches.

Installing Extra Closet Shelving

Stuff You Need to Know

Toolbox:
- Stud finder
- Pencil
- Measuring tape
- Level
- Drill
- Drill bits
- Screwdriver

Materials:
- Wall shelf (with mounting hardware)

Time Needed:
Less than an hour

Kids' rooms contain stuff they no longer use (although hopefully you've gotten rid of these items in your preliminary sorting), stuff they use right now, and stuff they will use . . . someday. The "someday" items are my focus with this project; they may include hand-me-downs that the kids haven't grown into and toys you're saving for later.

I recommend storing "someday" items in the least-accessible portion of the bedroom because they're off-limits or not used on a regular basis. The top portion of a child's closet, above the clothing rod, is ideal.

Measure the dimensions of the available space above the clothing rod so you can buy the correct number of shelves in the right size. Measure the available height from the top of the rod to the top of the ceiling; the available depth from the front closet wall to the back closet wall; and the available length from the inside left wall to the inside right wall. Note any closet features that would hinder installation such as light fixtures, clothing rod brackets, or recessed areas.

Purchase shelves with the maximum possible dimensions for your space. You can buy shelves up to ½ inch less than the available depth of your space, and I recommend purchasing shelves with a width about 6 inches less than the available width of your space to allow some wiggle room when locating wall studs. If you're working with 12 to 36 inches of vertical height, I recommend adding a single shelf. If you have more than 36 inches of vertical height at the top of the closet, you can easily add two shelves; allow at least 18 inches of vertical distance between shelves.

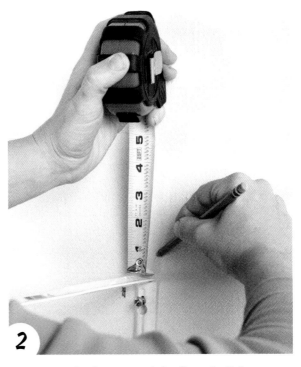

Determine the location of the first shelf. I recommend hanging it as low as possible, ideally a few inches above the clothing rod. Use a pencil to mark this height along the studs.

Use a stud finder to locate a wall stud in the back of the closet above the closet rod, and mark in pencil. Measure 16 inches to either side to locate and mark an additional wall stud. Repeat along the span of the closet wall where the shelf will be hung.

Your child's closet may have a shelf with hanging space instead of a rod. You can easily adapt the instructions in this project to work for the space above the existing shelf.

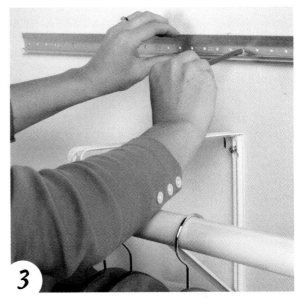

Hold the shelf up to the wall so that the hanging mechanisms align with your stud marks from Step 1, and use a pencil to mark through the screw holes to indicate where you'll drill holes.

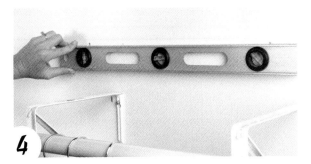

Use a level to ensure that the spots you marked in Step 3 are level.

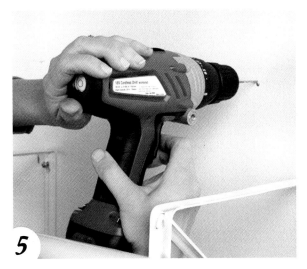

Using a drill bit that's slightly smaller than the screws required for the hanging mechanism, drill holes in all the marked spots, applying consistent horizontal pressure.

TIP

Want a clever use for extra closet shelving in your child's room? Divide your child's toys into three or four groups, and store each collection in a large plastic box on the shelving. Once a week, substitute a new box of toys for an old box. Your child will delight in a new box full of surprises, and you'll watch in amazement as old toys become new again.

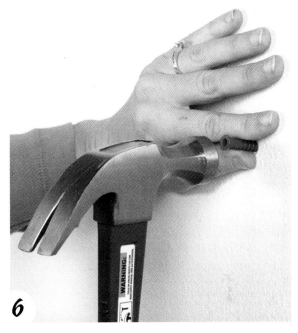

If you're unable to drill into a wall stud, reinforce the installation by using drywall anchors. Simply position the drywall anchor into the predrilled hole and tap with a hammer until the anchor is almost completely in the hole.

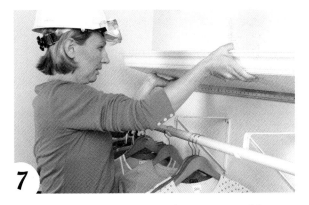

Use a screwdriver to insert the screws and hang your shelf. Repeat this process for additional shelves.

Creating Under-the-Bed Rolling Storage

A twin-size bed in a child's room provides more than 15 square feet of storage underneath the bed! By adding stackable, readymade bed risers (available in home stores) to the feet of your child's bed, you can add anywhere from 1 to 7 inches of height. With a custom storage unit, you can maximize this area to store books, bedding, toys, dress-up clothing, shoes and socks, or bulky items like sleeping bags or luggage. The storage unit box that you create in this project will free up tons of closet space and floor space!

Before you run out and buy any supplies, measure the width, length, and height of the space underneath the bed to determine how much space you have. Note that the box will need to slide in and out between the risers. For the width, measure the available space between the risers or bed legs on the left and right side of the bed; for the length, measure the available space between the risers or bed legs at the head and foot of the bed; for the height, measure the usable space between the floor and the bottommost portion of the bed frame. Keep an eye out for any features of your bed that would prohibit under-the-bed storage or at least prompt adjustments in the size of your storage box, such as a support leg in the center of the bed frame.

After you've determined the under-the-bed dimensions, plan the dimensions of your box so you can buy the right amount of wood. You may want to subtract 2 inches from the width measurement so that your child doesn't bump his or her toes on the box when making the bed, and you should subtract 1 inch from the length for "wiggle room" and 3 inches from the height measurement to account for rolling casters. Then, pick the closest size of standard wood board without going over. Everybody has heard the term *one by four,* or 1x4, which refers to a piece of hardwood (like oak) or softwood (like pine) lumber (not plywood) with specific measurements: As detailed in Chapter 3, the "four" refers to the width of the piece, and it's actually 3½ inches wide instead of 4 inches. The same goes for *one by six, one by eight,* and so on — they're all ½ inch less than the listed width. The standard wood board width choices for this project are 4, 6, 8, or 10 inches. For example, a 10-inch high space under the bed minus 3 inches for casters is 7 inches, so you'd use the next lowest standard board size, a 1x6, which is 5½ inches wide. Here's an example of dimensions for the space under the bed and for the box to help you get your numbers straight:

> Dimensions of available space under the bed: Width 38 inches, length 73 inches, height 10 inches

> Dimensions for the under-the-bed box: Width 36 inches (reduced by 2 inches), length 72 inches (reduced by 1 inch), height 7 inches (reduced by 3 inches), wood board 1x6

When you have the dimensions of your box planned, it's time to shop for your wood. You need a base piece of ½-inch plywood to match your width and length dimensions; two 1x6 pieces of wood board to match your length dimension; and two 1x6 pieces of wood board to match your width dimension minus 1½ inches (to accommodate the corners of the box). Here's a wood supply list for the example dimensions:

> ½-inch plywood, dimensions 36 x 72 inches

> 1x6 wood board, two pieces each cut to 72 inches long

> 1x6 wood board, two pieces each cut to 34½ inches long (allows for the thickness of the corners)

1

Lay out the length pieces and width pieces in a rectangular formation. Add wood glue to connect the width piece and the length piece, and quickly position them together. (You can apply glue either to the end of the width piece or the side of the length piece.) Repeat with the other end of the width pieces and the other length piece.

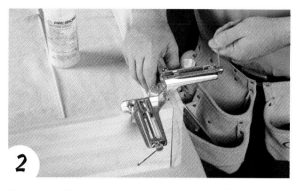

2

Connect all corners with clamps, and allow approximately two to three hours for the glue to dry. Leave clamps on for Step 3.

3

Reinforce the corners with nails. Turn the rectangular frame on its side, and if the clamps don't interfere, use your nail gun or hammer to nail two to three nails through one end of a length piece into the width piece at the corner. Repeat on the remaining corners, and then remove the clamps.

If you're unable to nail because of the type of clamp you're using, remove one clamp and nail through one end of a length piece into the width piece at the corner. Repeat on the remaining corners, removing one clamp at a time.

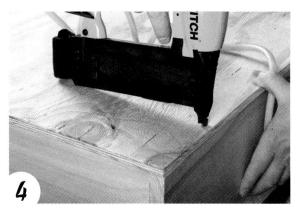

4

Lay the frame on the ground so that the sides are vertical and the bottom edge is facing up. Position the base sheet of plywood on top of the frame. Use a nail gun or hammer to drive nails through the base into the frame pieces. Hammer in two to three nails at every corner and at 6- to 12-inch increments along the width and length pieces to securely connect the base to the frame.

5

While the unit is upside-down, position four casters on the bottom corners of the base. Each caster should have four screw holes, so locate your casters so that three of the four holes align with length or width frame pieces. Use a pencil to mark where you'll drill your screw holes.

6

Using a drill bit that's slightly smaller than the screws required for the casters, drill holes in the 16 marked spots, using consistent vertical pressure.

7

Screw the casters onto your base. For each caster, use 1-inch screws for the three screws installed into the wood board frame pieces, and use ½-inch screws for the single screw installed into the plywood. You use shorter screws for the plywood so that you don't get a sharp screw poking up through the bottom of the storage box.

8 Flip your box over, fill it up, and roll it under the bed.

The Finishing Touches: Reassembling Your Kids' Space

After you've installed one, some, or all the projects that appear earlier in this chapter, it's time to put your kids' space back together again! The following sections provide some inspirational ideas for pint-sized storage pieces and furniture arrangements.

Using 4-x-4 storage units

The best organizational item I own is a 4-x-4 storage unit. As the name implies, this unit has a frame with 16 individual storage cubbies, and each cubby has about 1 cubic foot of storage (see Figure 9-1). You can customize each cubby with bins, drawers, or doors, or you simply can leave it as open storage. Available at many home stores, this unit is a workhorse, and if you're willing to scale back your children's toy collections, it can store all their toys, books, and more.

Figure 9-1: A 4-x-4 storage unit has room for toys, books, crafts, and more.

A few of my favorite uses for this unit are

✔ **A bedroom divider:** Use your 4-x-4 unit to separate the sleeping part of a child's bedroom from the play area.

✔ **An organizer in a playroom:** Your 4-x-4 unit can hold toys, books, craft supplies, diapering supplies, and games. Small children can't reach the upper cubbies, making them a great place to stash items that aren't childproof.

✔ **A toy cubby underneath a loft bed:** You can store all your child's toys and books in the 16 cubbies, and placing it under a loft bed is a great use of space. As your child grows and you add a desk under the loft, use the 4-x-4 unit to store books and desk supplies.

Bolt the unit to a wall to prevent tipping.

Go, Van Gogh, go! Stocking an art cart

Kids (and those of us who are kids at heart) love arts and crafts. Experimenting with different textures like fabric, feathers, and foam enhances fine motor skills and is just plain fun. Let your children's imaginations run wild by providing them with a child-size craft station in a four-tier rolling cart with drawers. You won't believe the results!

I recommend providing a wide variety of craft supplies, but don't overdo it. Stick to items that are easy to sweep up or vacuum. Years of being a "Craft Mom" have taught me to just say no to glitter glue, stamp pads, Play-Doh, and very small beads. Nobody likes to pick Play-Doh out of the carpet!

Group items into logical categories, one per drawer:

✔ **Base:** The foundation of a craft project includes construction paper, white paper, coloring pages, foam frames, wood frames, and wood hearts or other shapes.

✔ **Accessories:** The things kids can adhere to the base include feathers, pipe cleaners, pompoms, beads, and stickers.

✔ **Tools:** The things kids use to manipulate materials include safety scissors, hole punchers, stencils, rulers, and glue sticks.

✔ **Coloring:** You guessed it! The items in this category include washable markers, colored pencils, and crayons.

Fill up your craft cart and label each drawer. If your child can read, use word labels. If your child is learning to read, use a visual cue (such as a picture of scissors) and a word label ("Scissors") for each drawer. Talk to your children about how this is their craft cart and they're in charge of putting items back in the proper drawers. Kids love the responsibility and structure of ownership!

Locate your craft cart next to a small work table in your children's bedroom or playroom. Provide age-appropriate sample projects from magazines to inspire your children, and let their imaginations soar. Enhance this space with a bulletin board to display their masterpieces!

Outfitting a "coffee corner" for reading

A funny thing happens when I'm in a preschool, church nursery, or playcare environment — I end up sitting on little chairs at a little table with little people. I don't know how the teachers manage to work all day in this miniature environment, but it sure does suit the needs of children.

My church nursery has what's referred to as a "coffee corner." I laughed at this description, but it's true! Coffee houses have perfected the technique of creating a cozy grouping of armchairs, small tables, and magazine/newspaper racks. The nursery has a kid-sized version of the "coffee corner," and the kids love it!

Create a "coffee corner" in your child's playroom or bedroom by following these simple steps:

1. **Start with an area rug, and position it a few inches from the corner of the room.**

2. **Add two kid-sized armchairs; opt for the medium version rather than the tiny version so that adults can be reasonably comfortable on these chairs, too.**

3. **Add a small square coffee table-like workspace that can be used for games, art, puzzles, or free play.**

4. **Mount a magazine rack on the adjacent wall to hold a collection of books.**

5. **Mount wall cubbies or shelves to hold games, toys, and supplies.**

Hang tight! Expanding closet rods

I love to see the determination on a toddler's face as he climbs up a step stool and grabs a cup from a cabinet that's beyond his reach. It would have been easier for him to ask for help, but children have an innate need to be productive people and do it themselves.

This same principle applies to getting dressed each day. Young children, particularly girls, love to pick out their clothes each day and dazzle you with their combinations of cowgirl hat, princess dress, and rain boots. Even though their outfits may not match, children will appreciate your words of affirmation as they show off their ensembles. Support your youngster by adding a lower clothing bar to the closet. Children's clothing is very short, so you can easily double hanging space in the closet. A lower bar allows your child to easily access her own clothing and help put away her laundry. The following solutions are both easy and temporary so that you can readjust the closet as your child grows:

✔ Purchase closet rod expanders or doublers at home organization stores or large home stores. The standard models can expand from about 20 inches to 35 inches wide and hang below the higher closet rod at a height of 28 to 50 inches. You simply customize the width and height of the expander, like you would a tension rod, and connect the unit to your existing rod with the hooks provided (check out Figure 9-2).

✔ Create your own lower rod by hanging a shower rod or dowel from your upper rod. I recommend connecting the two with a rigid material like heavy-gauge wire so the lower rod doesn't swing.

Figure 9-2: Let your kids reach their own clothes with a closet rod expander.

Chapter 10

Learning to Love Your Laundry Room

Sort, empty pockets, spot treat, wash, dry, hang, fold, press, repeat. The process of doing laundry is a rhythmic cycle of incoming dirty items and outgoing clean items. Like ever-forming laundry piles, laundry rooms are very predictable — you're not going to find a small home office or a reading nook tucked in this space! Laundry rooms are for doing laundry, plain and simple. They're generally small spaces, but with a few simple enhancements they can do big things! This chapter helps you free up your crowded laundry room by wall-mounting ironing boards and drying racks and adding a clothing line. I also address storage and organization of cleaning supplies in wall cabinets. Trust me, no sock is left unturned!

The goal of your laundry room is a serene space where you accomplish all tasks involved in cleaning clothes. Your laundry room may have limitations standing in the way of this goal, such as a small size, limited air flow, or lack of storage. Furthermore, most households are guilty of laundry-related items winding up in other parts of the house. It's not uncommon to see piles of folded clothes on a sofa, an ironing board propped up against a bedroom wall, or clothing draped on a treadmill. Although you may enjoy performing mundane laundry-related tasks in the living space of your home, these items are an eyesore and a constant reminder of laundry. And it's unfair to blame your missed treadmill workouts on your unorganized laundry room! If you can accomplish your sorting, cleaning, folding, and ironing in the confines of your laundry room, you save a lot of scurrying-around time and preserve the serenity of your living spaces.

Because the laundry room is generally isolated from the living spaces of your home, it usually isn't a catchall for stuff like most rooms in the home. In fact, laundry rooms are generally *missing* key components like irons, ironing boards, and laundry baskets! After you know your laundry room's goal and limitations, it's time to empty, sort, and retrieve missing things. Transfer the entire contents of your laundry room to an adjacent room — this can be accomplished in minutes — and sort it into the following four categories:

✔ **STAY:** This item is in good condition, is used often, is relevant to the goal, and will stay in the laundry room. Most items fall under this category, such as detergent, spot treatment, bleach, and laundry baskets.

✔ **MOVE:** This item is in good condition and is used often, but it should be moved to the linen closet or bedroom. Examples include towels, sheets, and pillowcases as well as items that have crept into the room like children's toys, work projects, and your secret stash of holiday gifts!

If you own a cat (or two or three), remove the litter box from the laundry room! Animal scents don't enhance the path to clean clothing. Litter boxes are ideally located in a garage, separate mudroom, covered porch, or other space not associated with cleaning or food preparation.

✔ **SHARE:** This item is in good condition but hasn't been used in the last year, is a duplicate, or no longer serves the laundry room's goal. Examples are extra linens or duplicate laundry accessories like hampers or ironing boards. Donate these items to charity, or put them in your next garage sale.

✔ **GO:** This item is trash! Examples include used dryer sheets or cleaning products that are expired or empty.

After you sort the contents of your laundry room, go on a scavenger hunt to collect missing items that actually belong in the laundry room! Gather up your iron, ironing board, starching products, and that pile of clothing you were getting around to pressing.

Select the projects from this chapter that will help you maximize the storage in your small laundry space. When you're done, check out the section "The Finishing Touches: Reassembling Your Laundry Room" at the end of this chapter for ideas on maintaining your laundry room's newfound organization.

A family affair: Having your kids help with laundry

Whether you're carting around your chubby cherub in a basket of clean towels or nagging your tween to put away her clean clothes, getting the kids involved in the laundry process is important and will cut down on your workload in the long run. You can even make it fun by following these tips:

✔ A basket of clean laundry is a tactile experience for infants who can sit up unassisted. Plop your little one in the laundry room next to you and watch him dig through the basket of clean clothes. You can probably fold an entire load of laundry while he's occupied with new textures.

✔ Toddlers love to dump and sort. After clothes have completed the spin cycle in the washing machine, dump damp clothes into a laundry basket on the floor and have your toddler fill up your dryer. Add encouragement and clapping and your dryer should be filled up in . . . about ten minutes. It may not be faster than doing it yourself, but it will save your back in the long run! (Note: Remove crackers and action heroes before running the dryer.)

✔ Preschoolers are learning to be independent, and you can help by giving yours the task of putting away her socks, underwear, pajamas, and anything else that doesn't require hangers. If she's determined, she'll do a pretty good job of folding too!

✔ Children in grade school can read and multiply, and in my book that means they should be able to put away their own laundry. Ensure that dresser drawers are easily accessible and clothing rods are at a child's height to assist your child in this task. (See Chapter 9 for ideas on organizing kids' closets.) Reinforce the message by teaching your child that if he wants to look nice for school, it's his job to bring dirty clothes to the laundry room and put his clean clothes away.

✔ Around the time the hormones kick in, adolescents should be fully in charge of their laundry. Start early and stick to your guns so you don't end up being the parent of the college kid with pink socks and underwear!

Installing a Retractable Clothesline

Stuff You Need to Know

Toolbox:
- Measuring tape
- Pencil
- Drill
- Drill bits
- Screwdriver

Materials:
- Retractable clothesline (with mounting hardware)

Time Needed:
Less than an hour

According to my home's resident laundry expert — my husband — the most frustrating part of doing laundry is trying to find a spot to hang garments that are drying. Items hanging from doorways or in hallways drip onto the floor and often fall off the hanger. Fortunately, my home's resident organizer — me — has a quick fix: a retractable clothesline! This handy device spans the length of one wall of your laundry room and can hold a basket's worth of laundry. You simply pull the clothing line from the main wall bracket and connect it to the receiver wall bracket. When not in use, the line retracts and is concealed inside the main bracket. No more trail of drying garments littering your doorways, hallways, and bathrooms!

Purchase a clothesline that's at least as long as the wall parallel to where you'll hang the line. I recommend hanging your line parallel to the longest wall available; you'll mount the brackets on the two walls adjacent to the long wall.

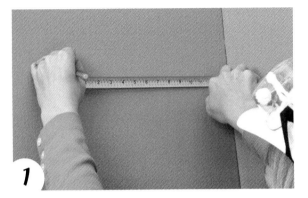

Grab your measuring tape and determine the exact location of the brackets on your walls. I recommend locating them high enough to accommodate hanging garments — 65 to 75 inches from the floor should do the trick.

Also, determine how far away from the longest wall you want to install the brackets. If you intend to dry your clothes on hangers, make sure the line, when extended, is at least 12 inches away from the long wall to accommodate standard hangers. If you intend to use clothespins, you can locate your brackets closer to the long wall.

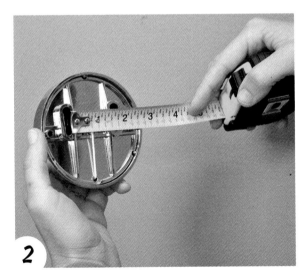

Measure the distance between the screw holes on the main bracket and transfer this measurement to the wall at the height determined in Step 1. Note that some models allow you to stick a pencil through the bracket to mark where you'll drill holes.

Hold the receiver bracket up to the opposite wall directly across from the main bracket. Use a measuring tape to measure down from the ceiling and in from the corner to make sure that your brackets are in the same place on opposite walls. Use a pencil to mark through the screw holes to indicate where you'll drill holes to mount the bracket.

Using a drill bit that's slightly smaller than the screws required for installing the brackets, drill holes in all the premarked spots, applying consistent horizontal pressure.

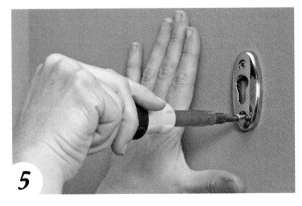

Use a screwdriver to screw both the main and receiver brackets to the wall.

Installing an Accordion Drying Rack

If you don't have an entire wall to dedicate to drying laundry, consider a wall-mounted accordion rack. This gadget looks like a towel bar when retracted and expands outwards in an accordion fashion to hold items while drying. An accordion rack is also handy to have over a laundry room sink so drips can go directly into the basin.

Because your rack will hold up to 20 pounds of laundry, you need to install it into at least one wall stud.

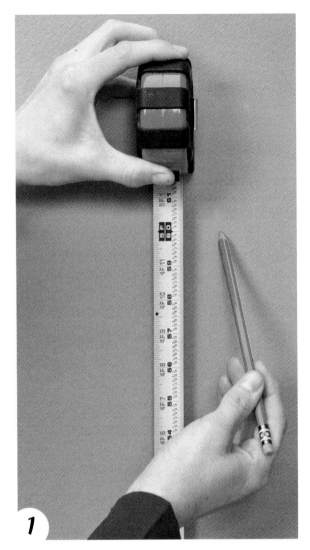

1

Determine the location and height of your drying rack. I recommend locating it on a side wall or over a sink at about arm-level height (around 55 to 60 inches from the floor) to lessen any strain on your back, but the height is purely personal preference. If you have curious little children, you may want to install it at your eye level (60 inches or more from the floor) so that the kids won't mistake it for a set of monkey bars.

Use your measuring tape and a pencil to mark the wall at your desired height.

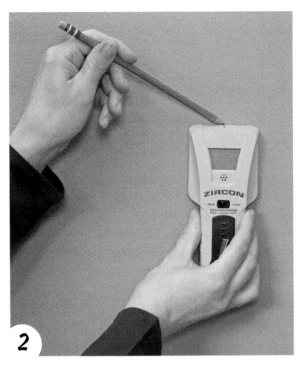

2

At your marked height, locate a wall stud with a stud finder (as I describe in Chapter 3) and mark the spot in pencil.

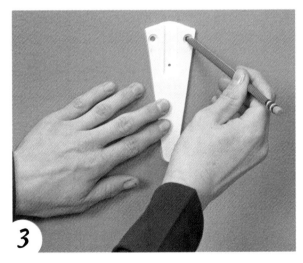

3

Drying racks are typically wall-mounted using two detachable brackets. Hold one bracket up to the wall along the wall stud at the spot determined in Step 2. Stick a pencil through the screw holes on the bracket to mark the wall. These marks indicate where you'll drill your holes. Repeat for the second bracket.

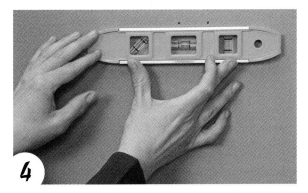

4

Use a level to ensure that the screw marks for both brackets are level.

5

Using a drill bit with a slightly smaller diameter than the screws required for the brackets, drill holes in all the marked spots, applying consistent horizontal pressure.

6

If the placement of your rack means that you're only able to mount one bracket into a wall stud, strengthen the installation of the other bracket by adding drywall anchors. Simply position the drywall anchor into the predrilled hole and tap with a hammer until the anchor is almost completely in the hole.

Adding a drying rack over the sink cuts your cleanup in half after a day at the beach, pool, or even running through sprinklers in the yard. While your washing machine is happily humming along with a load of grimy towels, transfer your clothes from the dryer to a retractable clothing line (a project I describe earlier in this chapter) and load your hand-washed bathing suits onto the accordion rack to drip-dry over the sink. (Does this mean you can cool off in the water twice as long?)

7

Align the screw holes of the brackets with your predrilled holes, and screw the brackets to the wall with a screwdriver.

8

Attach the accordion rack to the brackets by snapping or sliding it in place or by twisting in small screws provided with the kit.

Note: Some accordion racks come with a second set of brackets so you can use the same accordion rack in a second location, like the bathroom, simply by unhooking it from the brackets.

Refreshing your laundry room's décor

Life is messy. Mess creates laundry. Laundry is reality. Now that you've come to terms with the rhythm of laundry, you can make the experience as enjoyable as possible. Here are some tips for revamping your laundry room's look:

✔ Zen or zippy? Paint your laundry room to reflect how you want to feel in this space. Light blue and sage green create a soothing, peaceful space that will help you get into the rhythm of folding. Vibrant yellow, orange, and fuchsia will add zip to the time you spend sorting. Crisp navy or red stripes create a tidy look and may help you iron those creases extra straight.

✔ Soothe your subconscious. Use scented plug-ins or scent diffusers to mask the chemical smell of your space. The scent of lavender will calm you, and citrus will make you smile. When purchasing detergent, select a scent that you love, or opt for unscented products.

✔ Still bored? Why not add a radio, MP3 player, or wall-mounted TV to enhance your time in this space? (Adding an additional phone line *may* be taking this concept too far!)

✔ Do you have the right light? If you find that you've missed a stain or two, consider increasing the wattage of your light bulbs or adding an additional light source.

✔ Is your room a comfortable temperature? Set up a circulating fan to keep you cool.

✔ If you tire easily, add a small chair or stool to use while sorting or ironing. Additionally, a padded rug or gel mat will reduce leg strain if you stand up to do your work.

✔ Don't forget to outfit your room with a small trash can for dryer sheets and lint.

Mounting a Fold-Away Ironing Board

If you don't *want* to iron a shirt, you probably don't *have* to. You can invest in wrinkle-free fabrics, embrace (or start!) the "slightly wrinkled" trend, use a wrinkle-release product, or frequent dry cleaners. You also could remove one item from your dryer at a time and race to hang it on a hanger before it wrinkles.

For most folks, ironing is a way of life. Why not indulge your love of ironing by adding a full-size, wall-mounted ironing board? The main benefit of a wall-mounted board is that it stays in your laundry room — and enables you to wash, dry, iron and fold all within the confines of this space. Think about how much time you'll save by completing all your laundering tasks in a single space. When not in use, the fold-away ironing board folds up against the wall and doesn't take up any valuable square footage like a free-standing ironing board.

1 Determine the wall location of your ironing board. When the board is down and perpendicular to the wall, it shouldn't interfere with loading the washer and dryer, block the doorway of the room, or trap you in a corner. Your ironing board also should be near an outlet. If you have a positioning preference because you're right-handed or left-handed, take this into account too!

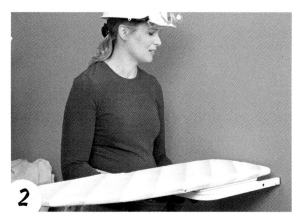

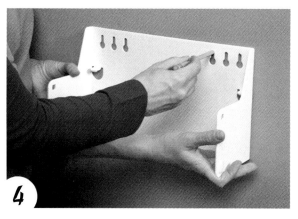

Determine the height of your ironing board. Are you tall or vertically challenged? Do you intend to iron sitting down or standing up? If you want to stand and iron, the board should be between waist height and chest height, depending on your preference. If you want to sit and iron, figure out the height of your board while sitting on the stool or chair that you'll use. Use your measuring tape and a pencil to make a note of your desired board height in the location where you'll hang it.

Hold the hanging mechanism up to the wall vertically along the wall stud. Adjust the height of the board so that the bottom of the board lines up with the mark made in Step 3. Use your pencil to make a mark through the hanging mechanism to show you where to drill your holes. (If the holes in the hanging mechanism are blocked by the ironing board, detach the board from the hanging mechanism and then mark the holes.)

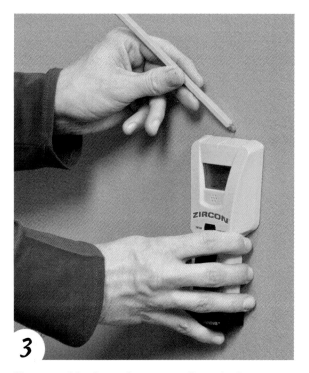

Neglected irons, like many household devices, pose a potential fire hazard. Consider installing a smoke detector in your laundry room to protect your family and home.

Use a stud finder to locate a wall stud where you intend to hang your ironing board (see Chapter 3). Use a pencil to mark the stud at the height determined in Step 2.

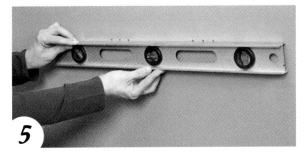

5

Use a level to ensure that the marks made in Step 4 are even.

7

Ironing boards are generally very heavy. If some or all of the bracket holes aren't in a wall stud, strength the installation by inserting drywall anchors. Simply position an anchor into a predrilled hole and tap with a hammer until the anchor is almost completely in the hole.

6

Using a drill bit that's slightly smaller than the screws required for the hanging mechanism, drill holes in all the marked spots, applying consistent horizontal pressure.

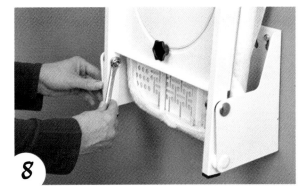

8

Attach your hanging mechanism to the wall by inserting the screws partway into the wall with a screwdriver, sliding the mechanism onto the screws, and fully tightening the screws. (Some models require you to align the screw holes on the hanging mechanism with the holes in the wall and screw the unit in place using a screwdriver.) If necessary, reattach the ironing board to the hanging mechanism with a wrench or small screwdriver.

Hanging a Wall Cabinet for Laundry Supplies

Stuff You Need to Know

Toolbox:
- Measuring tape
- Pencil
- Stud finder
- Level
- Drill
- Drill bits
- Screwdriver

Materials:
- Wall cabinet (with mounting hardware)

Time Needed:
Less than an hour

Your laundry arsenal may go far beyond detergent and bleach to include specific stain removers, color-safe bleaches, brighteners, whiteners . . . and the list goes on. Most laundry rooms have a horizontal surface such as a ledge or shelf on which to store cleaning products, but if you don't have this or just need more space, adding an all-purpose wall cabinet can really clean up your space!

I recommend selecting a sturdy cabinet from a home improvement store. Ideally, the cabinet will have two doors and, if you like, an adjustable shelf that allows you to accommodate items both large (detergent bottles) and small (dryer sheets). Measure your tallest item, and ensure that your cabinet can easily accommodate this item.

Make sure that a wall-mounted cabinet won't be a hazard to all who enter; laundry rooms are tight spaces, and heads can easily get bumped.

1

Determine the location and height of your wall cabinet. The area above the washer, dryer, or sink is ideal because this space otherwise would be unused. If you're installing your cabinet over a top-loading washing machine or dryer, make sure the bottom of the cabinet is high enough that you can still open the machine door; around 20 inches of clearance is usually safest.

If you're installing the cabinet on the opposite wall from your machines, consider the head-bumping hazard factor of upper cabinets in tight spaces and install it so that the bottom of the cabinet is close to your height. Make sure that you can access the contents at whatever height you choose. If your cabinet is over a flat surface like a table or counter, you don't have to worry about this hazard and can install your cabinet at a more comfortable height, with the bottom of the cabinet a few inches below eye level.

Factoring in all these considerations, mark the ideal height of the bottom of the cabinet on the wall with a pencil.

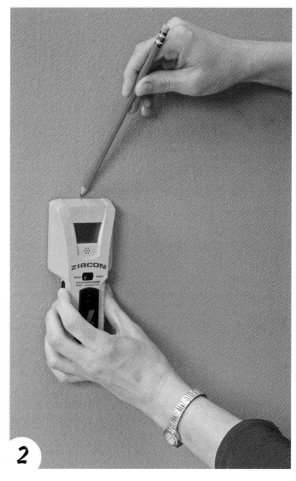

2

Use a stud finder to locate a wall stud and mark it at the height determined in Step 1.

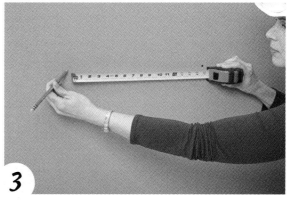

3

Measure and mark a second wall stud 16 inches away from the first stud.

Use a level to ensure that the pencil marks made in Steps 2 and 3 are at an even height.

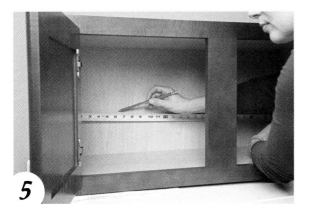

This installation requires drilling through the back of the cabinet and into the wall studs. Measure and mark two points that are 16 inches apart inside your cabinet. Ensure that the marks are centered on the back of the cabinet and level with each other. (For example, if your cabinet is 29 inches wide, subtract 16 from 29 so you have 13 inches total outside of the marks, or 6½ inches on each side.)

Align the marks on the inside of your cabinet with the pencil marks made on the wall in Steps 2 and 3. (You may need a helper to hold the cabinet in place.) Using a drill bit that's slightly smaller than the screws required for this installation, drill holes in all the marked spots, applying consistent horizontal pressure. Drill two to three holes per wall stud to support the heavy weight of the cabinet, and then screw the cabinet into the wall studs.

Detergent bottles are known to drip! Line the bottom of your cabinet with a heavy duty shelf liner to protect it.

Setting up a sewing station

Think your laundry room can handle more? If space permits, consider expanding your laundry room to include a sewing station for mending and other sewing tasks.

Begin with a sturdy, all-purpose rectangular table that has access to a wall outlet and doesn't interfere with your laundry, ironing, and drying racks. Mount a wall cabinet above the table (refer to the project "Hanging a Wall Cabinet for Laundry Supplies"), and add a comfortable chair. Position your sewing machine on the table, and fill your upper cabinet with your sewing kit, current projects, and supplies. Add an "Inbox" for all the incoming pieces of laundry that need repair. The hum of the sewing machine should mix well with the rattle of the dryer!

The Finishing Touches: Reassembling Your Laundry Room

After you've installed one, some, or all the projects that appear earlier in this chapter, it's time to implement some organization techniques that help you keep loving your laundry room. These sections provide some inspirational ideas for keeping the flame alive.

Sorting your laundry

Laundry can be intimidating. Perhaps you were the kid in college with the pink socks. I wasn't that girl, but I did date that guy. To avoid laundry mishaps, have everyone in your family deposit their dirty clothes into three bins in your laundry room labeled "Lights," "Darks," and "Delicates." The size of these bins depends on how much space you have available in your laundry room and how often you do laundry (translation: how much the bins need to hold). I recommend using medium-size wire bins that hold about one load of laundry each — give or take. When a bin is full, it's time to do a load. Purchase bins small enough to fit in your space but large enough to meet your laundry needs.

Here's how the bin contents should break down:

- ✔ **Lights** are anything that you can bleach and wash with hot water. Examples are socks, men's and children's underwear, and preshrunk light-colored cotton t-shirts. You can wash light-colored towels or linens with your light clothing or separate them to prevent the transfer of fuzzy material from your towels to clothing.

- ✔ **Darks** are almost everything else, and they should be washed in cold water. You can wash dark-colored towels with darks or separately from other laundry to prevent the transfer of fuzzy material from your towels to clothing. Wash new, brightly colored towels by themselves the first time to prevent bleeding. You also can sort out black items to prevent fading and wash with a special detergent made for black clothing.

- ✔ **Delicates** are garments that need to be hand-washed and air-dried and are generally of the female persuasion. This includes delicate garments such as women's underwear, bras, bathing suits, and nightgowns. Make sure all bra and bathing suit hooks are closed, and put all delicate items in a mesh bag to prevent them from snagging or hooking onto anything else.

If you plan to separate your towels or linens from your clothing on a regular basis, consider adding a fourth bin labeled "Linens." As with most home organization routines, do what works for you!

Before beginning any load, transfer items piece by piece from the bin to the washing machine. Check each garment for loose buttons, rips, and stains; set those that need mending aside in your sewing "Inbox" (see the earlier sidebar "Setting up a sewing station"), and treat stains before washing with a stain remover. Don't forget to remove all loose items from the pockets — you don't want to see what a single crayon can do to a load of laundry! And keep in mind that just because your family drags items into the laundry room doesn't mean they can stay; return loose items to each family member's room as you return their clean laundry. Staying organized takes discipline!

Stashing a few tools for folding and storage

Outfitting your laundry room with the following tools will minimize your folding and storing time:

- ✔ **Use a flip-fold laundry board.** Available online or at as-seen-on-TV merchants, laundry lovers swear by this product! Use the board to help fold laundry and get perfectly folded clothes and towels every time.

   Alternatively, you can fold clothes on your wall-mounted ironing board, counter, or side table.

- ✔ **Manage your hangers.** Keep an extra supply of plastic hangers in your laundry room on a wall-mounted hook (see Chapter 7 for the basics on mounting a hook), and use them for clean clothing that needs to be hung. Each time you grab a load of laundry from your bedroom closet, grab a stash of hangers to restock the laundry room. This will save you many trips back and forth!

- ✔ **Return clean clothing piles to each family member's room.** And if children are old enough, let them put away their own laundry. By seeing how much effort goes into putting clothing away, they'll be less likely to throw clean items in with the dirty clothes.

Chapter 11

Giving New Life to Your Garage

Tasks performed in this chapter

✔ Hanging a pegboard to store tools

✔ Installing a ceiling rack

✔ Mounting a bike lift

✔ Creating a zone for sports equipment

Kitchens are for cooking. Bedrooms are for sleeping. Living rooms are for living. What are garages for? Traditionally, garages were for parking cars, of course. They were man-spaces with oil spills on the floor, clunky wood workbenches, and tons of greasy tools. They stored items like fishing poles, lawnmowers, and gardening tools.

Not anymore! Garages no longer have such a defined function. Instead they serve as a catchall for the items that don't fit in the rest of your home. Today's garages can take on any of a number of personalities; here are just a few that may apply to your garage:

✔ Old school garage: A place to park your car and hang your hammer.

✔ Artist's studio: A room dedicated to painting, ceramics, crafting, or gardening; vast amounts of tools and supplies and not a car in sight!

✔ Busy family: A space filled with balls, bats, bikes, backpacks, skis, roller skates, and more; a hard-working room that has to accommodate warehouse-quantity home goods (like a 24-pack of toilet paper and 12-pack of paper towels), your kid's science project volcano, and pet food.

✔ Lounge: The look and feel of an indoor room, complete with flooring, furniture, painted walls, and media.

✔ Garage band: A space dedicated to everything teen!

If your garage is anything like mine, it's a combination of the preceding garage personalities. Each homeowner has distinct needs, and each garage is unique. The goal of this chapter is to equip you with all the know-how and ideas to create your ideal garage based on the limitations of your space. This chapter encourages you to declutter your garage, mount your equipment and tools on the wall, stow your seasonal storage overhead, and create clever systems for dealing with all your supplies. Trust me, you *will* see your garage floor again!

So what are some typical limitations of a garage? The most common is the amount of space that can actually be devoted to storage! As families grow and their needs evolve, the garage is often the first room to be converted into a hobby room, teen hangout, or workshop. In colder climates, it's often necessary to park your car in your garage, which leaves even less room for storage. Further limitations include temporarily storing items for kids away at college, using your garage as a stock room for your home-based business, or . . . not having a garage at all! This chapter details several creative storage solutions that you can put to use in whatever garage space you have available.

By now the creative juices should be flowing! You're developing a visual of your ideal space, and you're going to channel that energy into emptying the garage and sorting through your stuff. Move the entire contents of your garage outside (if weather permits) or into an adjacent room. This crucial step allows you to assess what you have and enables you to quickly eliminate items that don't support your goal. This task may seem daunting, but you can accomplish it in less than half a day.

Garages hold enormous amounts of stuff. I recommend sorting your items into four large piles labeled as follows:

- **STAY:** This item is in good condition, is used often, is relevant to the goal, and will stay in the garage. Examples are sporting equipment; tools; and automotive, cleaning, and pet supplies.

- **MOVE:** This item is in good condition and used often, but it doesn't belong in the garage. For example, seasonal clothing can be transferred to your closet, and borrowed items should be returned to friends and family members. (Don't they have their own garages?)

- **SHARE:** This item is in good condition but hasn't been used in the last year, is a duplicate, or no longer serves the garage's goal. Examples include boxes of old clothing, extra kitchen items, old sporting equipment, and furniture you're unlikely to use again someday.

- **GO:** This item is trash! Examples are broken furniture, damaged items, and empty cardboard boxes.

Creating a cleaning caddy

How do you clean your house? If you tend to do frequent five-minute touch-ups or have few bathrooms, you may keep cleaning supplies in each bathroom and under the kitchen sink for easy access.

In most situations, people keep household cleaning supplies in one central location and use a portable caddy to travel with certain supplies from room to room. This approach is recommended if you have many bathrooms to service and it's hard to stay on top of stocking each room with supplies.

The garage is the ideal spot to keep your household cleaning supply stash and cleaning caddy. Start with a large plastic tub, and fill it with the following items:

- **For the bathroom:** Tile cleaner, mildew cleaner, toilet bowl cleaner, and soap scum remover

- **For the kitchen:** Disinfectant spray, granite cleaner if you have granite countertops, and stainless steel cleaner if you have a stainless sink or appliances

- **For the floors:** Spot treatment, floor cleaner, and floor polish

- **For general purposes:** Window cleaner, all-purpose cleaning spray, scratch-free cleansing powder, ammonia, goo remover, baking soda, vinegar, bleach, leather cleaner, and clean rags (which are more environmentally friendly than paper towels)

Purchase a large cleaning caddy that has a handle; I recommend using a plastic caddy because it's waterproof and easier to clean than a fabric one. Store the caddy in the garage with your cleaning products until the time comes to load it up with what you need to clean a particular room or surface in the house. For safety purposes, locate the caddy on an upper shelf or in a upper cabinet.

Fixing up an empty garage

Does your space have that new-garage smell? It's not often that you find yourself with a completely empty garage! Embrace this rare opportunity by touching up the walls and floors. Reframe the way you think about your garage: If it looks more like a finished interior room, you're more likely to keep the space tidy and organized.

1. **Evaluate your space and divide it into zones.**

   ✔ Measure your available wall space and interior space. Storage should be on the perimeter of your garage. Estimate if and where you'll park your car, locate your workbench, and place any lounge furniture.

   ✔ Determine which types of items you'll store in your garage, and carve out your zones. Examples of zones are garden, car parking, sporting equipment, mudroom, pet center, workbench, and crafts.

2. **Finish your concrete floors by trying one of the following techniques:**

   ✔ Cover your concrete floors with laminate peel-and-stick tiles. They cost about $1 per square foot and provide a durable surface that you can still park your car on.

   ✔ Buy a large area rug from a remnant warehouse, and add a mesh anti-slip mat underneath to help the rug stay in place.

   ✔ Enhance the look of your floors with concrete paint or epoxy. Select a color that sets the tone for your space: Aqua adds a "wow factor" to a lounge, beige complements a calm gardening space, and red energizes a teen's garage band. (On second thought, maybe you shouldn't choose red!)

3. **Beautify your walls.**

   ✔ Remove all hardware (nails, hooks, and screws) from your walls.

   ✔ Repair any holes, cracks, or imperfections.

   ✔ Add a fresh coat of paint. If you're striving to make your room to feel like part of the home, select the same color as the adjacent room. You may already have a gallon of this paint on hand anyway!

   ✔ If you plan to devote your garage to a few main zones, paint each a different color to emphasize the utility of each space. For example, try a garden zone painted green with a framed picture of a thumb for inspiration!

4. **Wrap up with finishing touches.**

   ✔ Lighting is essential for a workspace. Use this opportunity to add extra overhead or task lighting to your garage.

   ✔ Return to your garage any workbenches, shelving units, and storage carts that support your goal and organization plan.

People love to hang on to old furniture, and it usually ends up gathering dust in the garage. You may have wonderful intentions of refurbishing that old cabinet or fixing the broken leg on the chair, but if it just isn't getting done, consider donating these items to charity. They'll be refurbished and used rather than just take up space in your garage.

After you sort your garage's contents, choose the projects that will help you store what's in the "STAY" pile, and get to work! When you're done, check out the section "The Finishing Touches: Reassembling Your Garage" at the end of this chapter for ideas on maintaining your garage's organization.

Hanging a Tool Pegboard

Stuff You Need to Know

Toolbox:
- ✔ Measuring tape
- ✔ Pencil
- ✔ Level
- ✔ Drill
- ✔ Drill bits
- ✔ Screws with heads larger than the holes in the pegboard
- ✔ Screwdriver

Materials:
- ✔ Pegboard (with spacers)
- ✔ Pegboard hooks or pegs (for hanging tools)

Time Needed:
Less than an hour

A toolbox is great storage device for do-it-yourselfers and carpenters on the go. It has a handle for easy transportation and can accommodate small items like hammers, screwdrivers, wrenches, wire cutters, nails, and screws. But where do you put your 4-foot level?

A garage tool rack is a great supplement or replacement for a toolbox! Pegboard tool racks are constructed from wood, plastic, or stainless steel and can hold large items like drills, saws, and levels. When you're working on a project, small items like hammers and screwdrivers hang at arm's length.

Hanging a large item such as a pegboard by yourself can be challenging, so you may want to recruit a friend to help with this installation.

1

Select a location for your pegboard that's above your workspace. If you stand at your workbench, locate the top of your pegboard a few inches above eye-level. If you sit at your workbench, locate the bottom of your pegboard flush to your work surface. Use a measuring tape and mark your chosen height with a pencil.

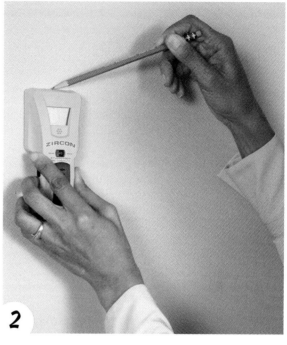

2

Locate a wall stud in your chosen location with a stud finder, and mark it with a pencil.

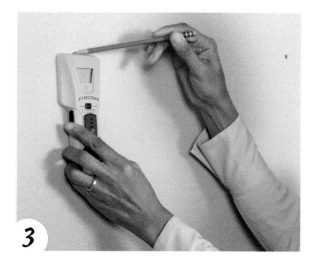

3

Locate and mark additional wall studs 16 inches to either side of the first wall stud.

4

Most pegboards don't have a hanging mechanism or bracket, so you have to drill through the pegboard into the studs. Hold your pegboard up to the marked wall studs and push a pencil through the pegboard holes you'll hang it from to indicate where you'll drill holes. If your pegboard spans multiple studs, reinforce the strength of the installation by marking drill holes in both the top and bottom of each stud.

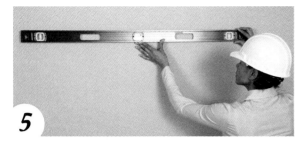

Use your level to check the heights of the marked holes and verify that the pegboard will hang level.

Ensure that your screws are narrow enough to fit through the pegboard holes but have heads larger than the pegboard holes. Using a drill bit that's slightly smaller than the screws, drill holes into the wall studs at the marked spots, applying consistent horizontal pressure.

Position the pegboard against the wall and have a helper hold it securely in place. Place a spacer between the wall and the pegboard at each drilled hole, and insert the screws through the pegboard holes and spacers into each drilled hole and screw them in with a screwdriver. (Spacers provide a gap between the wall and the pegboard for the back ends of hooks and pegs used for hanging tools.)

Outfit your pegboard with hooks or pegs on which to hang your tools.

As your tool collection grows, reconfigure the storage hooks or add a second pegboard rack to accommodate your expanding collection.

Installing a Ceiling Rack

Stuff You Need to Know

Toolbox:
- ✔ Ladder
- ✔ Measuring tape
- ✔ Stud finder
- ✔ Pencil
- ✔ Drill
- ✔ Drill bits
- ✔ Screwdriver
- ✔ Wrench and bolts needed for certain kinds of racks

Materials
- ✔ Ceiling rack (with mounting hardware)

Time Needed:
Less than an hour

Sometimes, wall storage in your garage isn't enough, and you need to bring out the big guns: ceiling racks! Ceiling racks are great for storing large or infrequently used items, and they're accessible by a ladder. A standard size rack is 4-x-8 feet, which translates to 32 square feet of floor space. Multiply this number by the distance from the rack to the ceiling, and your new storage area will rival that of a walk-in closet!

You mount the frame of the unit into ceiling joists using attached brackets, and the base connects to the frame. Installation is very simple . . . the hard part is deciding how to fill up your new storage space!

Grab a helper because this is a two-person job. You're working with multiple pieces overhead and up on a ladder.

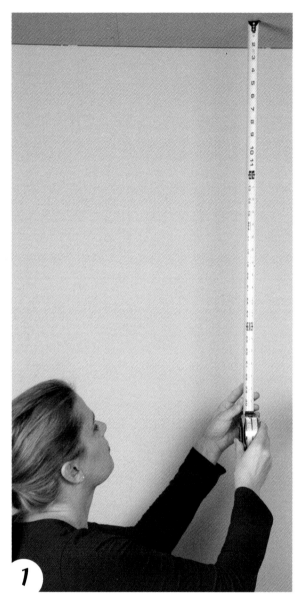

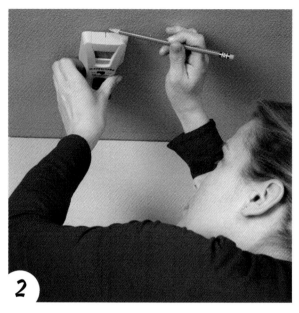

While you're on a ladder, use a stud finder to locate a ceiling joist in the area where you want to hang your rack. Note whether the joists run north-south or east-west, and mark them with a pencil. (See Chapter 3 for an introduction to ceiling joists.)

Move 16 inches in the appropriate direction (determined in Step 2) to locate additional ceiling joists with a stud finder, and mark them with a pencil.

Determine the location of your ceiling rack. Open ceiling space is best, but note that you also can install a ceiling rack in the unused space between your garage door rails and your ceiling. Get on a ladder and use a measuring tape to ensure that there's enough vertical space (at least 36 inches) to locate your rack here and that it won't interfere with the operation of the garage door.

If you have low garage ceilings with less than 36 inches of clearance between the rails and ceiling or any other obstacles that would interfere with a rack, you should locate your ceiling rack on the opposite end of the garage.

4

Hold the frame of the rack up to the ceiling and mark the locations of the bracket mounting holes along the joists with a pencil.

5

Using a drill bit that's slightly smaller than the screws provided for this installation, drill holes in the marked spots, applying consistent vertical pressure.

REMEMBER

Use your ceiling rack storage area to house items that you need to access infrequently. This is a great place for your turkey deep-fryer because nobody minds climbing a ladder before Thanksgiving dinner, but resist the temptation to store your lawnmower up there! Camping equipment, holiday items, and long-term storage paperwork are also perfectly at home on ceiling racks.

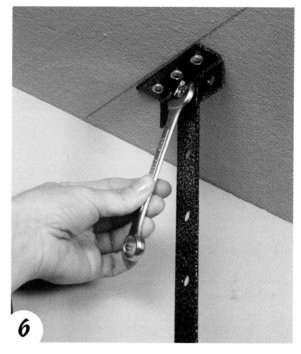

6

Screw the brackets into the ceiling using a screwdriver. Use a screwdriver or wrench, depending on the model, to connect the frame to the brackets.

7

Complete the installation by attaching the grid to the rack by snapping or screwing it in place. Then load up your rack!

Mounting a Bike Lift

As gas prices soar, people are turning to their bikes as an excellent way to cut down on the high cost of gasoline, squeeze in a little exercise, and have fun while doing it. Another perk of biking? You never have to circle for a parking spot!

Bicycles are typically stored in the garage to prevent rust and corrosion. Bike lifts free up valuable garage space by raising the bike to ceiling height with a lift that attaches directly to the ceiling. The lift holds the handlebars and seat of your bike, and a pulley system helps you lower or raise your bike. Bike lifts are great for homeowners with high ceilings in their garages or for those who rarely use their bikes.

Overhead installation is always cumbersome, so grab a helper for this installation!

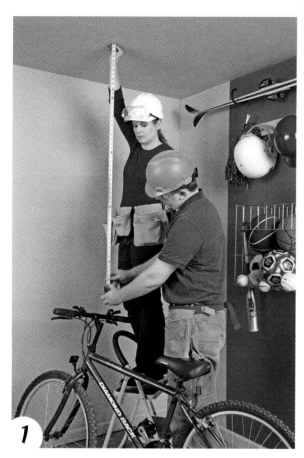

Determine the location of your bike lift. Your bike will hang approximately 48 inches from the ceiling, so pick a spot where the bike won't interfere with a walkway, workbench, or the garage door. Get up on your ladder and measure 48 inches down from the ceiling in your chosen spot to ensure you have enough room.

Do you know that a bike lift can accommodate items other than bikes? Consider installing a lift to store bulky items like strollers, lightweight gardening equipment, and camping gear. Make sure the item you plan to hang is stable enough to be supported by two hooks.

Use a stud finder to locate a ceiling joist that's far enough from the wall it faces that the tires won't bump into the wall. This distance is approximately 16 inches for standard adult bikes, but you will want to verify this measurement for your own bike. Mark the location with a pencil.

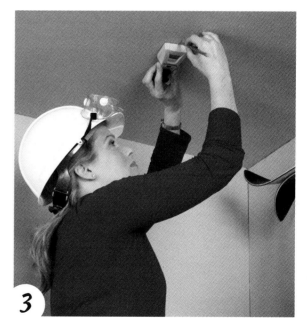

Determine if the ceiling joist found in Step 2 is running the length of your bike or perpendicular to the length of your bike (north-south or east-west). If the joist runs the length of your bike, you don't need to find any additional joists. If the joist runs perpendicular to the length of your bike, measure 16 inches away from the first joist to locate and mark additional ceiling joists. Three should do it!

Hold the seat hanging mechanism up to the first ceiling joist found in Step 2, and mark through the screw holes on the bracket to indicate where to drill your holes.

Determine the location of your second hanging mechanism, which holds the handle bars. If you're working with multiple joists, I recommend using the third ceiling joist (two away from the one marked in Steps 2 and 4) because the distance from the bike handle bars to the back of the seat is about 32 inches, which is exactly equal to the distance between the first and third joists. (If you're working along a single joist, you can just measure 32 inches along the joist.)

Hold the handle bar hanging mechanism up to this location and mark through the screw holes on the bracket to indicate where to drill your holes.

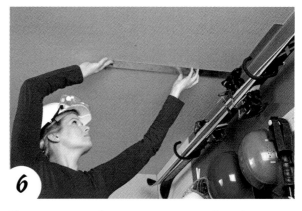

Use a carpenter's square to ensure that the marked spots for both hanging mechanisms are perpendicular to the wall of your garage.

Using a drill bit that's slightly smaller than the screws required for the hanging mechanisms, drill holes in the marked spots, applying consistent vertical pressure.

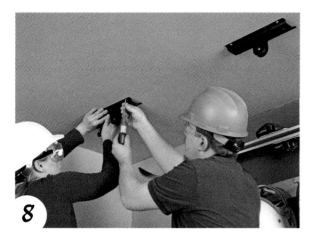

Screw the hanging mechanisms into the ceiling joists using a screwdriver. You may want to have one person hold the bracket against the ceiling while the other person screws it in place.

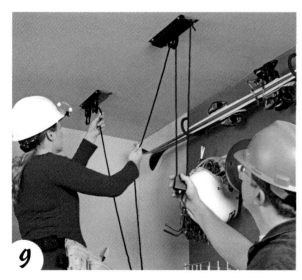

Connect the clamps and pulley system to the ceiling brackets.

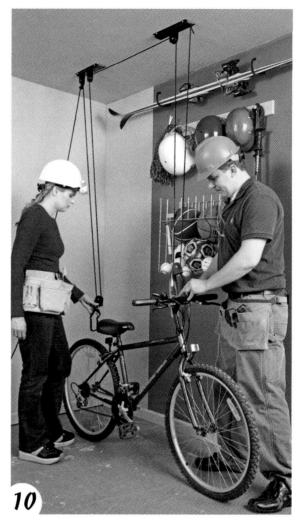

Attach the clamps to the seat and handle bars of your bike. Use the pulley system to lift the bike to the ceiling and free up some floor space. (Some models provide a hook that you can mount to the wall to hold the excess length of cord.)

If your family bikes frequently and you don't want to use a lift, you have other options for storing your bikes. Bike stands, for instance, hold bikes upright by trapping the front wheel. They're a great solution for children's bikes because kids can get their bikes in and out by themselves. Bike stands require light assembly but no installation; they simply stand on the floor. In addition, bike hooks and racks are ideal for storing teen or adult bikes. Bike hooks hold a bike by the tire, and bike racks support a bike under the carriage; both are mounted into a wall stud and can hold up to 50 pounds.

Creating a Zone for Sports Equipment

Stuff You Need to Know

Toolbox:
- Pencil
- Stud finder
- Drill
- Drill bits
- Screwdriver
- Level
- Measuring tape
- Drywall anchors

Materials
- Two strong twist-in hooks
- Peg rack (with mounting equipment)
- Sporting equipment cage (with mounting equipment)
- Jumbo clear plastic tub

Time Needed:
Less than half a day

Growing up, I played soccer, and my husband played basketball. We just assumed our kids would follow our lead and choose a sport with a nice round ball. So much for assumptions! Our kids love every sport and want to try a new one each season. They also love a variety of ways to get around town — scooters, skateboards, roller skates, inline skates, and even rolling shoes!

Although we enjoy our kids' enthusiasm for all things athletic, storing sporting equipment is taxing on the garage. Do you face the same dilemma? Why not create a sports zone in an unused area of your garage? You should allow at least 4 horizontal feet of storage space to accommodate storage components for all your sporting equipment.

Maximize your storage by dividing your sports zone into four layers. From top to bottom, I recommend a set of wall hooks to accommodate seasonal items like skis; a peg rack for helmets, jump ropes, and sports bags; a sports equipment cage to corral balls and bats; and a large sturdy tub to hold items like skateboards, roller skates, and tennis rackets. Add extra cages and tubs to suit the needs of your children.

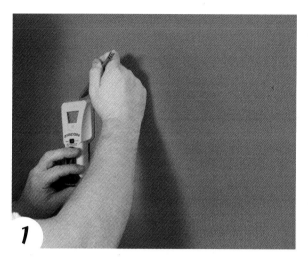

Determine the location of your sports zone, and locate four or more wall studs with a stud finder, marking them with a pencil. I recommend marking each wall stud in a few different spots, starting a few inches from the ceiling.

Using a drill bit that's slightly smaller than the screws on the twist-in hooks, drill holes in the marked spots (one hole for each hook), applying consistent horizontal pressure.

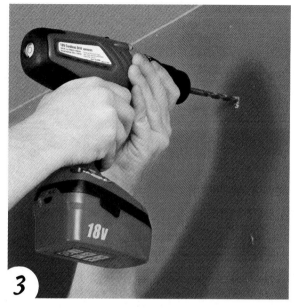

For the top level (wall hooks), use your measuring tape to mark 6 inches below the ceiling on the first and fourth studs (which should be 48 inches apart). If you plan to hang only children's skis, mark the first and third studs (which should be 32 inches apart).

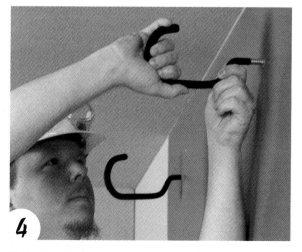

Twist hooks into the holes. If you have several pairs of skis or other seasonal equipment to hang, repeat to add more hooks 8 inches below the first set.

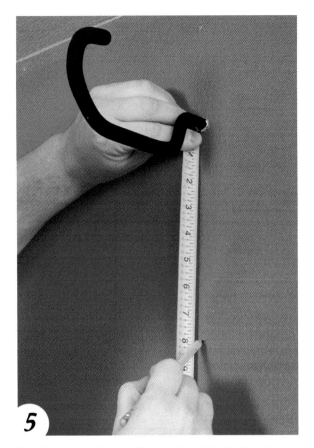

For the second level (the rack with individual pegs/hooks for hanging helmets, jump ropes, and sports bags), measure and mark two or three wall studs approximately 8 inches below the last row of hooks.

Hold your peg rack to the wall so that at least one hanging mechanism is in line with a mark made in Step 5. Use your pencil to mark through the screw holes of the hanging mechanisms.

Use your level to ensure that the pencil marks are even and the rack will hang level.

Using a drill bit that's slightly smaller than the screws required for the peg rack installation, drill holes in the marked spots, applying consistent horizontal pressure.

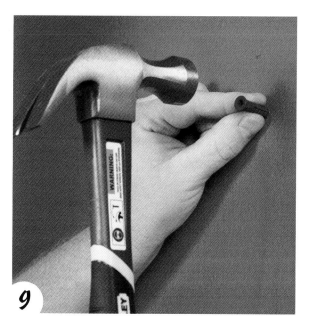

9

If one of your hanging mechanisms isn't in a stud, use drywall anchors to reinforce the installation. Simply position the drywall anchor into the hole, and tap with a hammer until the anchor is almost completely in the hole.

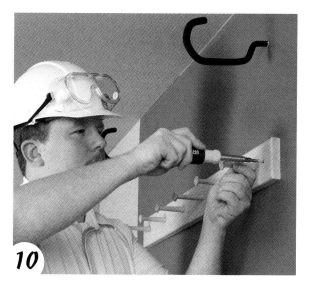

10

Hold your peg rack to the wall and screw it in place using a screwdriver.

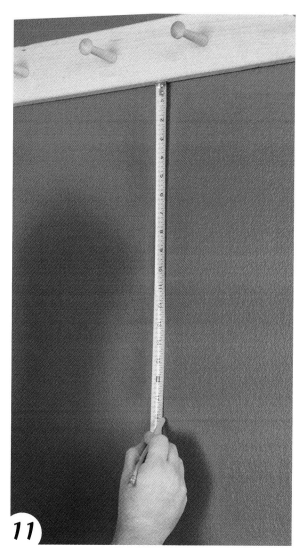

11

For the third level (the sports equipment cage), position the top of your sports equipment cage at least 18 inches below the bottom of the peg rack to allow for items like bike helmets hanging on the pegs. Mark the height of the cage on the second and third wall studs.

TIP

Involve your kids! After you put together your sports zone, have your children outfit it with their favorite gear. Ensure that the most frequently used items are placed at their height and less frequently used items (like skis) are stored toward the top.

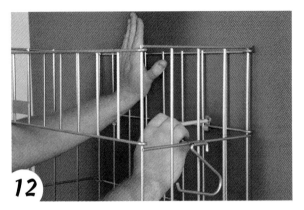

Hold the sports equipment cage to the wall in such a way that the top is at the height determined in Step 11 and the hanging mechanisms line up with the second and third wall studs. (Standard cages are 20 inches wide with the hanging mechanisms located 16 inches apart, so both hanging mechanisms mount into wall studs.) Stick your pencil through the screw holes of the hanging mechanisms to mark where to drill your holes.

Hold your sports equipment cage to the wall and screw it in using a screwdriver. You can hang a second cage below or next to the first cage by repeating these steps.

Use a level to ensure that the marks for both hanging mechanisms are level.

Using a drill bit that's slightly smaller than the screws required for the cage hanging mechanisms, drill holes in the marked spots, applying consistent horizontal pressure.

Slide an extra large, sturdy, plastic tub on the floor below the equipment cage to store equipment that's challenging to wall-mount, like inline skates, skateboards, and collapsible scooters.

The Finishing Touches: Reassembling Your Garage

After you install one, some, or all the projects that appear earlier in this chapter, it's time to put your garage back together again. The following sections provide some inspirational ideas for filling up all your new storage space!

How does your garden grow? Organizing your gardening supplies

An organized garden area will get you from your garage to your geraniums in seconds! Begin with storing your tools on the wall:

✔ Tall tools can be stored in a trash can dedicated to gardening, on a wall rack that grips the tools, or in sturdy wall-mounted hooks spaced a few inches apart.

✔ Small tools can hang from a simple peg rack or hook or be stored in a small bucket.

If you have a few shelves on a rack or in a cabinet that you can devote to small gardening accessories, great! If you're creating an entirely new area, position a simple wood shelf against a wall, and add a durable, washable area rug to define the space. Then customize your area by doing the following:

✔ Group loose seed packets in a zippered bag or waterproof box to prevent damage from moisture. Group your collection by planting season (later winter, early spring, and late spring), or alphabetize them for easy access!

✔ Nest ceramic pots so that they take up less space.

✔ Utilize a waterproof garden caddy for all your grab-and-go items, such as gloves, knee pads, and handheld tools.

✔ Stash a wide-brimmed hat and sunscreen near your caddy.

✔ Add a large plastic tub in the lower section of your storage area to corral dirty items, such as potting soil, outdoor shoes, knee pads, and gloves.

✔ Add a large plastic tub exclusively for poisonous items on the highest shelf or in a remote location that children and pets can't access. For safety's sake, the tub should have a locking lid and be labeled "Poisonous."

✔ Place a stainless steel trash can on the floor. It's a great home for tall, dirty tools, fertilizer, or potting soil.

Organizing your automotive supplies

By the time you trek through your house and garage to collect your glass cleaner, rags, chamois, dashboard protector, and handheld vacuum, wouldn't it have been easier to go to the carwash? Not anymore! And certainly not at the prices they charge! Save time and money by creating a custom car care caddy in your garage.

Start with a sturdy, rolling base. Folding carts, wagons, and tiered utility carts are good options. Purchase an item that's sturdy enough to hold tools, if necessary. Then purchase a large, round, plastic caddy that has a handle. Because you'll likely be doing automotive projects on your driveway, locate your caddy on the shelf nearest to the garage door that leads to the driveway. For safety purposes, locate the caddy on a higher shelf to prevent children or pets from accessing any dangerous chemicals or tools.

Purchase cleaning products and accessories specifically dedicated to car care:

- ✔ **Products:** Glass cleaner, all-purpose surface cleaner, carpet cleaner, and wax or polish

- ✔ **Cleaning implements:** Sponges, rags, chamois, squeegees, brushes, and old toothbrushes

- ✔ **Miscellaneous:** A handheld vacuum and extension cord

Place these items on your rolling base (except for the chemicals, which should be kept high up out of the reach of children and animals), and transfer only what you need to your portable caddy when you're ready to work on your vehicle.

If you perform your own oil changes and automotive repairs, create a service kit in your cart to reduce prep time; as with the items in the previous list, transfer only what you need to the portable caddy when you're ready to work on your vehicle:

- ✔ **Products:** Motor oil, replacement fluids, air filters, and other small replacement parts

- ✔ **Tools:** Wrenches, funnel, dipstick, and other car-specific tools

- ✔ **Miscellaneous:** Hand degreaser

Part IV
The Part of Tens

The 5th Wave   By Rich Tennant

"The funny thing is he's spent 9 hours organizing his computer desktop."

In this part . . .

The Part of Tens is a *For Dummies* tradition; in this part, I include two chapters, each with ten great tricks of the organizing trade.

You want to make a change, but you're too busy to tackle an entire room? Not in the mood to wield power tools? Look no further! Chapter 12 presents great organizing tips to make the most of your time.

Do you live in tight quarters? Check out the tips in Chapter 13 for living in tight spaces so you can make the most out of the space you do have. Enjoy!

Chapter 12
Ten Time-Saving Organization Tips

In This Chapter

Organizing rooms efficiently

Maintaining an organized lifestyle

It's my hope that this book dispels the common myth that organization takes too much time! By investing a few focused work hours now, you can shave minutes or even hours off your daily routine. This chapter provides ten tricks of the organizing trade that will help you complete tasks faster. The perk? You'll have more time for the things you want to do.

Keep Your Tools Handy

When you have a few room organizations under your belt, you see that the process doesn't take that long! You can further reduce the time it takes to transform a space by having your organizing tools ready to go when inspiration strikes. I recommend grouping your tools together in the following categories and keeping them in your garage to reduce your project prep time:

- **Sorting tools:** Stack your four sorting bins inside of one another, and tuck colored paper, markers, garbage bags, and lids into the bins.

- **Installation tools:** Create your own do-it-yourself tool kit to store the tools you most frequently use. This grab-and-go kit makes project installation a cinch!

- **Finishing tools:** Dedicate a space in your garage to finishing touches, such as bins, boxes, baskets, picture frames, candles, and vases. As you switch around your room décor, check out your garage stash before shopping for accessories. You may want to store your paint supplies in this area as well.

Flip to Chapter 2 for more details on gathering basic organizing tools.

Plan Convenient Spaces

Planning your spaces saves valuable time! When establishing the layout of a space, envision *how* you're going to work in the space. For example, set up your home office so that everything is at arm's length — you can type, answer the phone, use your printer, recycle, and access your files all without leaving your office chair. Here's another example: In your kitchen, locate frequently used items at eye level and rarely used appliances on upper shelves or in lower cabinets. Store your food in a cabinet or pantry that's within the *kitchen triangle* formed by the sink, refrigerator, and stove. Store less frequently used items, such as plastic storage items or specialty dishes, outside of the kitchen triangle.

Be Mentally Focused When You Organize

Are you inspired to tackle a room organization? Great! Clear your calendar and turn off your phone so you can really focus. You can accomplish more in one hour of focused work than in four hours of interrupted efforts. When you decide to sort through the mounds of items in a room, quickly sort items into their respective bins, and make quick decisions of STAY, MOVE, SHARE, or GO. Try to keep your STAY pile as small as possible by keeping only essential documents or items that you need to take action on. Remember that, if necessary, most information is easily found online. This isn't the time to contemplate old photos and letters and take a stroll down memory lane!

Stick to the Idea of "One In, One Out"

Organizing an entire room is a lot of work. After you've done the work and everything is in its place, you'll have a good idea of how much stuff the room can comfortably hold. If you don't curb your inflow of goods, it won't be long before you're right back where you started! Nip this vicious cycle in the bud by sticking to the principle of "One in, one out." If you buy a new picture frame, an old one has to go. The reverse, "One out, one in," also works; for example, if you break a lamp, you're free to buy another one to replace it. No fair breaking a lamp just to get a new one, though!

Repurpose Items

The needs of a household are ever-changing. There's a phase where your wardrobe takes center stage and a time when baby food jars need to be organized and accessible. Before long, you're into sports equipment, running a home-based business, and then back to the wardrobe. It's the cycle of life. While clever home organization stores sell a product for every need, repurposing your items as needs change is better on the environment and your pocketbook. There's no reason why a wood toy box can't be used for storing gardening tools or an old Ping-Pong table can't have a new life as an architect's drafting table or a place to spread out and work on crafts. If you have a keen eye and a bit of imagination, you can repurpose almost anything, and you'll save time and money, too!

Forget Spring Cleaning

Whoever thought of spring cleaning must have lived in one dirty place! Dirt, dust, clutter, and unnecessary items build up all year long. I like to do a quick decluttering of each closet in my house every few months. Logical times to tidy up your home are after the holidays, before summer, and before school starts. Hitting your closets at least three times a year helps you stay on top of clothes that are outdated or too small and allows you to rotate your seasonal items. To quote Benjamin Franklin, "An ounce of prevention is worth a pound of cure."

Make Time to Plan Your Day

Are you a morning person? Good for you! You can get up at 5 a.m. and have the day planned before your charges stumble bleary-eyed into the kitchen for waffles. If you do your best work only after you're fully awake, you should probably plan your day the night before. Get in the habit of taking a few extra minutes in the evening to review the next day's activities and obligations and prepare yourself. For instance, if I notice that I'm supposed to bring cupcakes to my daughter's class the next day, I'd rather shop for ingredients the night before!

Keep Plenty of Lists

Back in the old days, I never made lists. I roamed through stores searching for Christmas gifts, new shoes, or ingredients that would somehow come together to form dinner. If I forgot something, it was no big deal — I could always shop again the next day. Now that I'm a busy wife and a mother, I'm a firm believer in lists. Lists get the job done. You can organize them by store (grocery, home goods, home improvement) or by function (errands, gifts, projects). Find a list system that works for you, and stick to it! Whenever I find myself scraping the bottom of the jar of smooth peanut butter, I add it the grocery list immediately so my children don't have to suffer through a crunchy peanut butter and jelly sandwich. The horror!

Use One Central Calendar and Message Board

I recommend maintaining a single household calendar that encompasses work, school, sports, and church activities as well as other social engagements. If everything is in one place, you're less likely to have schedule conflicts or overlook hiring a babysitter. Here are a few suggestions for using a calendar and message board effectively:

✔ As events are added to the calendar, add related items to your to-do list or gift list.

✔ Post frequently used phone numbers like the local pizza joint and emergency contact/medical information.

✔ If you have room, tack up flyers, invitations, or coupons. Stay on top of coupon expiration dates or event dates to prevent your message board from becoming a clutter trap!

Don't have a message board? Fear not; I show you how to mount one in your kitchen in Chapter 5.

Pre-pack Bags for Last-Minute Events

Do you love spontaneity? Great! Embrace this character trait and prepare pre-packed bags so you can act on your spontaneity. Here are a few ideas:

✔ Fill a tote bag with towels, swimsuits, sunscreen, hats, toys, snack bars, and bottled water, and store it in your trunk in the summertime. You can hit the beach or pool at a moment's notice!

✔ Store your inline skates, protective gear, workout clothes, and a pair of socks in your car so a scenic drive can morph into an impromptu workout.

✔ Throw a wrapped hostess gift — something that won't melt or spoil, such as stationery, a picture frame, or potpourri — in your car for those times when a cellphone call leads you to a last-minute dinner party. Put a sticky note on the outside to remind you of the contents — just remember to remove it before giving the gift!

Chapter 13

Ten Tips for Maximizing Small Spaces

Are you in a small space by necessity or by choice? This chapter provides you with ten tips to organize the space you do have. Your cozy cottage or apartment will feel like a million bucks!

Incorporate Sneaky Seating

Add some sneaky seating to your living room by using storage cubes or ottomans. When not in use, they can store magazines, books, or toys, and serve as end tables. When guests come over, create conversation areas by strategically placing the cubes around the room.

Stash Discs in Media Folders

No room to store your CDs, DVDs and video game discs? Consider using media storage folders. I recommend one folder for each type of media, and don't forget to label them! (Chapter 4 has more information.)

Mount Your Kitchen Items on the Walls

Is your kitchen about to burst? Free up your pots and pans drawer with a ceiling-mounted rack. Want more? Pare down the contents of your utensil drawer with a wall-mounted rack. Still not impressed? Transfer spices to metal canisters on a wall-mounted magnetic strip. Not challenged yet? Eliminate your junk drawer by returning every item to its proper home. Gotcha! (Chapter 5 has a variety of kitchen projects.)

Use Double-Decker Storage

Shelf stackers double the storage of a kitchen cabinet by creating an upper level to hold a second row of cups or glasses. You also can load up a double-decker Lazy

Susan two levels high with spices or condiments and spin it around to find the right one. (Chapter 5 has details on kitchen gadgets.)

Make the Most of Your Table

How can you fit eight people at a six-person table? Consider a table with leaves to allow for additional seating. If you're not in the market for a new table, replace the chairs on one side of your table with a bench and squeeze in a few extra people.

Consider Clever Sleeping Options

In your grandparents' day, people raised a family of seven in a three-bedroom house. Plenty of families continue to make it work in small houses today. How? You can set up a bunk bed; loft the beds; or install a Murphy bed, which flips up inside a closet or wall unit.

Include Rods and Hangers in Your Closets

If you have a small closet, it's time to get creative! Try the following tips to get more items in your closet while keeping it tidy (see Chapter 6 for details):

- Suspend a lower clothing rod from your upper rod to increase hanging space.
- Mount specialty hangers on your wall to organize belts, ties, and scarves.
- Use pant/skirt hangers to hang up to five pants or skirts from a single hanger.

Hang Bathroom Items on the Walls

Running out of counter space in your bathroom? Maximize the space you have by wall-mounting your hair dryer, curling iron, and flat iron. Hang them from a rack or a series of hooks.

Build Under-the-Bed Storage

Want an extra 31 square feet of storage? Of course you do! Maximize the space underneath your bed by adding risers for extra height and using under-the-bed boxes. Chapter 9 shows you how to create rolling storage boxes using plywood.

Store Out-of-Season Items on Ceiling Racks

Are all your storage areas maxed out? Make the most of the height in your space by installing ceiling racks. They're great for storing holiday decorations or paperwork in the garage (see the project in Chapter 11) or off-season clothing in your closet.

Index